The Spirit of Excellence

RANDALL J. BREWER

CONTENTS

THE SPIRIT OF EXCELLENCE

INTRODUCTION

There are few figures in Scripture who model steadfast faith and unshakable integrity under pressure like Daniel. From the courts of Babylon to the den of lions, his story is a living testimony that God's power and sovereignty are not confined to holy places or favorable conditions. Daniel's life is proof that true faith can thrive even in exile, that holiness can stand strong in hostile territory, and that one person fully devoted to God can influence nations.

The Book of Daniel opens not in Jerusalem, but in Babylon. It begins with tragedy and loss — the fall of Judah, the destruction of the temple, and the forced deportation of young men of royal blood into a pagan empire. It is in this setting of defeat that Daniel's story begins, reminding us that God's purposes are not defeated when our world seems to crumble. Sometimes, His greatest works begin in our deepest trials.

Daniel was likely just a teenager when he was taken captive. Everything familiar to him — his home, his language, his culture, his worship — was stripped away. Babylon tried to erase his identity and reshape his convictions. He was given a new name, a new education, and a new environment. Yet what Babylon could not change was his heart. From the very beginning, Daniel resolved that he would not defile himself (Daniel 1:8). That single decision set the course for a lifetime of faithfulness.

In Daniel chapter 1, we see the foundation of Daniel's faith: a quiet but firm decision to honor God no matter the cost. He purposed in his heart to remain undefiled by the king's food and wine, not out of legalism, but out of devotion. His outward obedience was rooted in inward conviction. That kind of faith is not born in moments of crisis; it is forged in the daily choices of obedience long before the testing comes.

God honored Daniel's faithfulness by granting him favor and wisdom. Even in a foreign land, Daniel's faith made room for divine promotion. The world around him was dark, but Daniel shined as a light — not by blending in, but by standing apart. His story invites every believer to ask: *What is my Babylon, and will I stand faithful within it?*

By the time we reach Daniel chapter 3, we find his companions — Shadrach, Meshach, and Abednego — standing before a fiery furnace. The decree had gone out that all must bow to Nebuchadnezzar's golden image. Yet these young men stood tall while the world bowed low. Their faith was not theoretical; it was costly. They looked death in the face and declared, *"Our God is able to deliver us... but even if He does not, we will not bow"* (Daniel 3:17–18).

That is the kind of faith that heaven honors — faith that trusts God's power but does not demand His deliverance. Faith that remains faithful whether the outcome is miraculous or not. Their stand revealed a principle that Daniel himself would later live out: God's deliverance is not always from the fire, but often through it.

In chapter 2 and again in chapter 4, Daniel's gift of wisdom and interpretation comes to the forefront. When others panicked, Daniel prayed. When others feared, Daniel sought God. His calm confidence came from his unbroken communion with Heaven. Because Daniel stayed in touch with God, God entrusted him with revelation that no one else could receive.

This part of Daniel's story reminds us that spiritual insight comes not through intellect, but through intimacy with God. In a world filled with noise, opinions, and confusion, the Daniels of today must learn to hear Heaven's voice clearly. The wisdom that changed empires flowed from a man who refused to stop praying — even when prayer was outlawed.

By the time we reach chapter 6, Daniel is an old man — still faithful, still praying, still uncompromising. Empires had risen and fallen, kings had come and gone, but Daniel's character remained steadfast. When jealous officials plotted against him, Daniel did not fight to defend himself; he simply continued doing what he had always done: he opened his windows toward Jerusalem and prayed.

The lion's den was not the end of his story; it was the confirmation of it. Daniel's survival was not the result of luck or courage alone, but of a lifelong habit of trusting God. The God who shut the mouths of lions that night had been the same God who sustained Daniel through decades of trials. Faithfulness in youth had prepared him for faithfulness in old age.

Through it all, Daniel remained a man of influence — not because he sought power, but because he sought God. His integrity, humility, and faith elevated him in the eyes of kings. Nebuchadnezzar, Belshazzar, and Darius each encountered the living God through Daniel's witness. His life proved that even in a pagan government, one godly man can shift the atmosphere of a kingdom.

Daniel's story is not just ancient history; it is a prophetic mirror for our times. We too live in a kind of Babylon — a world that constantly pressures us to compromise, conform, and forget who we are in Christ. Yet like Daniel, we are called to stand firm, to pray boldly, to walk in purity, and to trust God's sovereignty even when the odds seem impossible.

The first six chapters of Daniel are not just about surviving captivity; they are about thriving in it. They show us how to walk in favor without losing faith, how to serve in secular places without being seduced by them, and how to remain holy in a culture that has forgotten what holiness means. Daniel teaches us that obedience brings influence, that prayer brings power, and that faithfulness brings favor — not always immediately, but inevitably.

As you journey through the story of Daniel, prepare to be challenged and inspired. His example calls us to a higher standard — one of courage, conviction, and consistency. It reminds us that when the world bows to idols, God still has people who will stand tall. When the lions roar, God still delivers. And when kingdoms fall, His Kingdom still stands.

The message of Daniel is you can live faithfully in a faithless world. You can stand firm when others fall. You can serve God boldly even in Babylon — and see His glory revealed in your lifetime.

| 1 |

"THE SPIRIT OF EXCELLENCE"

The life of a believer is more than accepting Jesus just so you can go to heaven. No, Jesus saved you so you can work with Him to help make the lives of other people better. God is calling you to make this world a better place and it takes godly character to do that. Therefore, the greatest call in all the world is to rise up and be a person with godly character. Believers with godly character embrace the call of God on their life, they're builders of other believers, and they reveal the Lordship of Jesus in their words and actions. They submit to the will of God as they allow Him to strengthen their soul and make them the person He created them to be. God wants you to live a successful life to the glory of Jesus Christ. He wants you to develop godly character so He can use you in a mighty way.

You become a person with godly character when you voluntarily surrender your will to do what's right in God's eyes, believing you'll receive His supernatural help along the way. The Greek word "charakter" means 'engraving, the figure stamped, an exact copy or representation.' It's translated in Heb. 1:3 as "the express image." Jesus is referred to as the "express image" of God. He fully represented the Father's nature, likeness, and character through His life. For this reason, Jesus could say, "He who has seen Me has seen the Father" (John 14:9). He then encouraged His disciples to learn from Him and follow His example. Christlikeness is your goal and destiny. One of God's primary goals for you as a child of God is to be conformed into the image of His Son. That's godly character.

Jesus Christ embodies all that is good. He is the perfect reflection of all godly qualities. It was Jesus who said, "You shall be perfect, just as your Father in heaven is perfect" (Matt. 5:48). The AMP Bible says you must be "growing into complete maturity of godliness in mind and character, having reached the proper height of virtue and integrity." The Message Bible says, "In a word, what I'm saying is 'Grow up.' You're kingdom subjects. Now live like it. Live out your God-created identity." Charles Spurgeon said you are to "stretch toward the highest conceivable standard, and be not satisfied till you reach it." All believers are called to be lights in this present darkness and the best light shines bright like the Father and gives glory to Him.

Since you're a child of a perfect Father in heaven, you are called to become perfect like Him. This is the goal you should always be striving to achieve. When God appeared to Abraham He said, "I am Almighty God; walk before Me and be blameless" (Gen. 17:1). MSG, "Live entirely before Me, live to the hilt!" The same call goes out to every believer today. The word "blameless" means 'complete; single-hearted; without blame; sincere; wholly devoted to the Lord.' John MacArthur said, "Because God is perfect, those who are truly His children will move in the direction of His perfect standard. If your life does not reveal growth in grace and righteousness and holiness, you need to examine the reality of your faith."

Matt. 6:33 says we are to seek first the kingdom of God "and His righteousness." We need to seek the righteous character of God and righteous actions toward people. As children of God, we've been created in His image and designed to reflect His character so that He is seen, enjoyed, and honored in us and through us. Paul told Timothy, "Train yourself to be godly" (1 Tim. 4:7 NLT). Godly character comes when you train yourself to focus on the kingdom of God and His righteousness. The great desire of the Father is that all believers would be conformed to the image of His Son, the only person who ever lived a perfect life. What God commands, He empowers and enables that it might be accomplished. Jesus said, "With men this is impossible, but with God all things are possible" (Matt. 19:26).

We can't be perfect on our own but with His help we can do anything. Gal. 5:16, "Walk in the Spirit and you shall not fulfill the lust of the flesh." It is Christ who empowers us by His indwelling Spirit to live the way the Father commands. It is in Christ that we are perfect in the eyes of God. Col. 4:12 tells how Epaphras always prayed "asking God to make you strong and perfect, fully confident that you are following the whole will of God." Heb. 13:21 (MSG) says Jesus will "provide you with everything you need to please Him, make us into what gives Him the most pleasure." TPT says He will "work perfection into every part of you giving you all you need to fulfill your destiny." ASV says He'll "make you perfect in every good thing to do His will."

Nothing you will ever do will be perfect but you must receive instead the perfection which God has already taken steps to provide for you. David said in Ps. 18:30,32, "As for God, His way is perfect. It is God who arms me with strength and makes my way perfect." It is God's responsibility to equip you to do His will and it's your responsibility to do it. God equips us but we must still do the work. We can't be perfect on our own but with Christ's help we can. Perfection is our goal, not for gaining salvation but for living the life of a born-again child of God. Having a godly character is what allows you to "walk in the light as He is in the light" (1 John 1:7). Yes, God is light and in Him is no darkness at all (vs. 5).

Although we may feel that we can never achieve the perfection of God, we are to forever seek after it and never be satisfied until we obtain it. Charles Spurgeon says we are to "rise out of ordinary manhood. Get beyond what others might expect of you. Stretch toward the highest conceivable standard." He also said, "Though you cannot be perfect, yet you must want to be perfect." The desire for perfection is what fuels your desire for godly character. A believer's life must exhibit maturity and progress toward the ultimate goal of perfection. Even when you miss the mark, the demand for perfection is still there. Spiritual maturity is not based on how long you've been born again, it's based on the level of your trust in God to make you a better person and a better believer.

Character matters because in life you will never rise above the level of your character. If you want to improve your life, you must improve your character. It's the level of your character that determines the level of your success in life, in ministry, in your work place, and in your relationships. The fulfillment of your destiny is based on the level of your character. If something is not right in your life, then something in your character is not right. What is godly character? In simple terms, it's doing what's right in any given situation. Your character is revealed in the way you deal with things. Godly character is when you do the right thing when nobody is watching. Never should you need an audience to do the right thing. God is the only audience you need.

Character in the life of a child of God is the constant manifestation of Jesus in the things they say and do. They will always be an imitator of the Lord Jesus Christ. Phil. 2:12,13, "Work out your own salvation with fear and trembling for God is working in you, giving you the desire and the power to do what pleases Him." MSG, "Be energetic in your life of salvation, reverent and sensitive before God. That energy is God's energy, an energy deep within you." God will work in you to improve your character at the level of your willingness to let Him do it. Therefore, submit to God and let Him have His way with you. In other words, God wants you to be consistently obedient by being continually dependent on Him. That's how you work out your own salvation.

Jesus said to "work while it is day" (John 9:4). Every day there is something you can do to work out your own salvation. There is either some sin to mortify or some grace to exercise. As you do your part, God will step in and do His part. The term "work out" means 'to engage in an activity involving considerable expenditure of effort.' It means 'to work out fully and thoroughly; to accomplish or achieve an end; to finish or carry something to its conclusion; to complete the effort and the work begun.' The life of a child of God is not a series of ups and downs but a series if ins and outs. God works "in" us and we work "out" what he has done in us. The Greek word for "work out" is "katergazomai" and it was used to describe working in a field with the reaping of a big harvest.

To be a person of character you must bring the whole purpose of your salvation to completion. Don't stop short of seeing the fulfillment of your very existence. Warren Wiersbe said, "God cannot shine through you until He works in you, so let Him have His way. You are a light in a dark world, a runner holding forth the living Word." Rejoice knowing God gives you the power and divine enablement to develop godly character. Your responsibility is to respond to God's ability working in you. God will not do the work for you for there is always a part you have to play. What He does do is supply the power that enables you to do what needs to be done. Charles Spurgeon said, "The assistance of divine grace is not given to put aside our own efforts, but to assist them."

Rom. 5:3,4 says we "glory in tribulations, knowing that tribulation produces perseverance; and perseverance character; and character hope." Paul is saying that joy, suffering, and perseverance produces godly character. Job was a man of character because he endured what he went through. So much was he a man of character that God bragged on him, saying, "There is none like him on the earth, a blameless and upright man, one who fears God and shuns evil" (Job 1:8). Job had character and God called him the finest man in all the earth. He was blameless, a man of complete integrity, a man who feared God. Endurance is the ability to stand up under adversity; perseverance is the ability to grow in spite of it. Therefore, out of patient endurance comes godly character.

A test is designed to determine the genuineness of the person being tried. Persevering when under attack becomes the grounds for gaining approval. James 1:12 says, "Blessed is a man who perseveres under trial; for once he has been approved, he will receive the crown of life." A person who has been approved is a person of character. Spiritual prosperous is the person who remains steadfast under trial. Forevermore that person will wear the crown of life. Enduring a test or trial promotes and validates the character of the person going through it. You have proof that your character is real for it has passed the test. When you courageously endure adversity and temptation, you'll come out the other side stronger and better and closer to God than you were before.

A person of character has within them a spirit of excellence. Dan. 6:3 says, "Daniel distinguished himself because an excellent spirit was in him." When one is distinguished, they are identified as being different and distinct from others. Daniel's spirit shined brightly in the dark world he lived in. Phil. 2:15 (NLT) says we are to "live clean, innocent lives as children of God, shining like bright lights in a world full of crooked and perverse people." The Hebrew word for "excellent" is "yattir" and it means 'greatest; preeminent; distinguished; outstanding; top tier; surpassing; superb; high quality.' Daniel's excellent spirit elevated him above everyone else. Your reputation is what people think you are, your character is what God knows you are.

God is an excellent God and everything He touches is done with excellence. To be a man of character you must, like Daniel, be a reflection of the excellent God inside of you. Daniel was a rare jewel, a man of integrity in a crooked and perverse generation. An ancient proverb says integrity is the first step to true greatness. His spirit was more excellent, more outstanding, and more superior than those around him. Spiritually speaking, he stood head and shoulders above everyone else. His heart and mind was of moral soundness and purity, of incorruptness, of uprightness, of honesty. He was a man of character. What you saw is what you got. He had a humble, holy, heavenly spirit. he had a devout and gracious spirit, a spirit of zeal for the glory of God and the good of men.

The excellence of a person is found in their character. They're a person of principle and integrity and is known for their honesty, ethics, and charity. Perfection and strength of character is our continual goal in this life. The truth be told, God is not satisfied with anything less than absolute perfection. A spirit of excellence overlaps into everyday life, so much so that every person you encounter recognizes there is something different about you. Excellence, by default, sets you apart from everyone else. You yield and become like the Lord, walking in excellence in everything you do. You're exceptional, a reflection of God and who He is. You are a person of character, an example for all the world to follow (1 Cor. 11:1).

In Matt. 6:10, Jesus taught us to pray to the Father, "Your kingdom come. Your will be done on earth as it is in heaven." Heaven is an excellent place and the world around you should be able to see the overlap of heaven in and through the excellence that radiates out of you. Excellence is beautiful in the eyes of God, so much so that He only allows His followers to excel to the altitude at which they align themselves with excellence. In other words, a person will never rise above their character. Without excellence there will be a big void in your life preventing you from reaching your full potential. You need to be full of godly character and the spirit of excellence so you can wholly and completely fulfill your destiny and be a reflection of who God is.

| 2 |

"CITY ON A HILL"

Every child of God on this planet has within them the divine spark of excellence that is forever waiting to explode into its full, brilliant potential. There is an appalling lack of excellence in the body of Christ because too many people are satisfied with being average and mediocre, for just being good enough. Their spiritual growth and heritage mean nothing to them, so they live beneath God's divine standard of excellence. It matters not that excellence is God's will for their lives. You need to come to grips with the fact that you are the creation of Almighty God and He made you to soar into the heavens on clouds of excellence and greatness. Living a life without limits is God's will for your life. The royal blood of heaven is flowing in your veins and you're to live the life of excellence and accomplishment.

2 Peter 1:5 says, "Add to your faith virtue." The word "virtue" means "excellence." The NLT says, "Supplement your faith with a generous provision of moral excellence." Peter is saying the first thing you do after getting saved is to pursue excellence

with all that is within you so that you can bring honor to your Father in heaven. Whenever a person properly fulfills their purpose in life they are referred to as a virtuous person, a person of moral excellence, a person after God's own heart. A person is excellent when they do what they are supposed to do, when they live their life to its full potential, when they run their race with their head held high. Those with a spirit of excellence live with a higher motive than others. Inside of them is the confidence that everything they do brings with it the possibility to glorify God.

Men and women of faith make active the excellence within them. They release it and let it shine as a light before others. They're like a city on a hill that everyone can see. When a person brings glory to God, they are fulfilling their purpose and thus exhibits excellence. They are faithfully doing what they were created to do. 2 Peter 14 says we are to "be partakers of the divine nature." That's excellence. This can happen because we possess the faith from which comes the divine nature of God. It is God's will for you to achieve and walk in excellence. Ps. 16:3 says, "And to the saints who are on the earth, they are the excellent ones, in whom is all my delight." Do everything with excellence. Col. 3:17 says, "And whatever you do in word and deed, do all in the name of the Lord Jesus, giving thanks to God the father through Him."

Don't live a mediocre life but let the divine spark of excellence within you explode outward toward everything you put your hand to do. Excellence is living to your full potential. It's submitting your will to the will of God. Ps. 37:23 says, "The steps of a good man are ordered by the Lord, and He delights in his way." Stop wasting time doing things that are mediocre and not necessary. Eph. 5:16 says to redeem the time. With excellence you're to make every second count. People with a spirit of excellence know there is no limit to what God can do through them. All God needs is your willingness to make it happen. God used a rooster to preach to Peter and a donkey to preach to Balaam. Surely, He can use you too. All you need is a fresh vision of God's power and who you are in Christ.

With excellence you can rise up and fly into your destiny, into the plan and purpose God has for your life. Take charge of your life and let God's will be done. Reject mediocrity and live a life with no limits, a life of abundance in God. Decide to live in a dimension of strength and power. Live with enthusiasm, vigor, and zeal. Never settle for being average for it is the grave excellence is buried in. Average people strive to fit in while excellent people strive to stand out. You can never change what you accept. Reject being average and mediocre and develop within yourself a deep commitment to excellence. You will never be excellent until you decide this is the lifestyle you want. Prov. 23:7 says, "For as a man thinks in his heart, so is he."

What you believe determines how you will behave. Integrity aligns your thoughts and words with your behavior. An excellent spirit is a spirit of integrity. Never ask God for excellence until you are first willing to go after it. Be consistent in your quest to be the best you can be. Be willing to go the extra mile. Strive for perfection. Strive for excellence. Always be faithful in doing what needs to be done. Never stop improving because excellence is a spirit that is never satisfied. Excellence is constantly growing. When you stop growing, you start dying. Be better than you were yesterday and tomorrow be better than you are today. Make excellence a lifestyle. Do things right the first time, all the time. Never do things halfway. Give it all you've got. Put your hand to the plow and never look back.

Excellence is not a gift. You are not born with excellence nor is it passed from one generation to another. Excellence is an attitude generated by a spirit. Excellence is not imposed from the outside, it is released from the inside. It affects how you talk, how you dress, how you organize your priorities. Those with a spirit of excellence have a higher standard of living than others. They will divide and conquer things that average people complain about. Most of the people who don't get ahead in life and don't fulfill their dreams are too busy complaining about why they can't get ahead in life. Excellent people pursue solutions while average people stare at their problems. What are you looking at? Are you looking at your problems or the God who is bigger than your problems?

Excellent people make improvements, not excuses. They pursue solutions to their problems, their obstacles, their challenges, and their opportunities. God is calling you to be a person of excellence, a person who doesn't only do what they have to do but always and without fail go the extra mile. They always do more that what is asked or required of them. They set a higher standard instead of following the mediocre standard that is in the world today. Jesus said we're in the world but not of the world (John 15:19). We can't be like everybody else.

2 Cor. 6:17 says we're to "come out from among them and be separate." Never doubt that with God excellence is the standard for how we are to live. Eccl. 9:10 says, "Whatever your hand finds to do, do it with all your might."

Hold nothing back. If something is worth doing, it's worth doing with excellence. Life is too short to just go through the motions of living a mediocre life. Solomon built the temple with excellence according to the blueprint God gave Him. Likewise, those with a spirit of excellence always follow God's blueprint for their life. People of excellence do what God wants them to do in the way He wants it done. Whatever you do, do it with integrity, character, godliness, and excellence. There are no shortcuts in the walk of excellence. Your life is only a vapor so make it count. Any endeavor you set out to do, give it everything you've got, and then some. Every day strive to live life more abundantly (John 10:10), to live an excellent life. Every day enjoy the presence of God who dwells inside of you.

Excellence cannot be measures or quantified. It is a spirit, an attitude. It's not found in comparison or competition. It's found in giving God the best you have. Excellence is a requirement for your dreams to come true. When others are preoccupied with things of this world, you are focused on having an excellent mindset. Average is not who you are. You are fearfully and wonderfully made (Ps. 139:14). Excellence is who you are and nothing short of that will do. People with spirit of excellence learn and grow from their mistakes. They become unique because they never quit and never give up on the dream in their heart. When excellence is your only option, you never stop moving forward. When life knocks you back one step, you grit your teeth and go forward two steps.

Grow from your failures and setbacks. From this day forward, make a conscious decision that excellence will be the description of everything you say and do. As you break through the barriers that stand in your way, you'll become more powerful than you were before. Your excellence is being nourished by the trials you overcome. Nobody is perfect but the spirit of excellence is. It's not about what you do, it's about what you become. If you become excellent internally, everything else will take care of itself. Put your heart and mind in motion and become hungry for excellence. If you'll hunger and thirst for excellence, you'll master your character and integrity. Let excellence flow through your veins. Let it touch everything you do. A football coach told his players, "How you do anything is how you do everything."

In other words, be excellent in every area of your life. If you have selective excellence, there is a malfunction in your character and integrity. Hold nothing back and be the best you can be knowing that excellence is what defines your true purpose in this world. It defines who you are and why you're here. You are a living, breathing miracle. You're made in the image of God. Every second you're alive is a gift so strive every day to be better than you were the day before. When life gets hard, work harder. Never make excuses. Face your challenges head on and conquer them. If you refuse to be average, you will prevail. If life you will struggle and sometimes you will fail. Never let these trials defeat you or define who you are. Make them building blocks to excellence.

Every day you'll face opportunities to compromise, to be less than what God made you to be. Shrug off the temptation to be average and keep pressing forward. Let the fact you've been called to excellence overshadow everything else. Never stop short of being the best you can be with the goal of getting better each and every day. Progress will be made but don't stop there. On the quest for excellence there will always be another mountain to climb, another challenge to overcome. Never lose sight of the ultimate goal of being perfect even as your Father is perfect. This is what validates your struggle and motivates you to keep pressing forward. It takes great determination to achieve excellence so you must always burn the midnight oil. While others are sleeping, you are forever striving to be the best you can be.

Excellence will never come to you, you must go after it. You must work hard for it. You must sleep excellence, breathe excellence, and eat excellence every single day of your life. Excellence will always be there waiting for you to grab onto it. Setbacks will come but the men and women of God use their failures to motivate them to press forward even harder. Achieving excellence is not easy and you must earn it with hard work, sacrifice, perseverance, and a whole lot of blood, sweat, and tears. It will be a struggle to stay positive and motivated but real men and women of God do it anyway. They don't look at the trial they're going through; they look at the goal they're going to. Constantly remind yourself that you are not yet where you're supposed to be but have the confidence that with a whole lot of grit and determination you've get there.

You've come a long way but the journey is not yet over. It's not that you haven't come far, it's that you haven't gone far enough. Excellence is not about being better than someone else, it's about putting forth maximum effort and giving God your very best, right here, right now. Make it your goal to pursue excellence and not success. Pursuing excellence will help you succeed, but pursuing success won't make you excellent. Anything done in the name of Christ should have excellence stamped all over it. Why? Because the nature and character of God defines and displays excellence. Make the pursuit of reflecting God's character through excellence your number one priority in life. 1 Cor. 10:31, "Whatever you do, do all to the glory of God."

God demands that you walk in excellence, that you give Him your best in all you do. By pursuing excellence, you glorify God and encourage others to live the same way. Pursue excellence in everything you do. Pushing the boundaries of your potential is what the spirit of excellence is all about. It's telling you to rise up and become more. A famous songwriter once said, "I'm not going to die with a song still in my heart." For sure, this person had the spirit of excellence. Excellence is about doing the best you can with what you have. It's about dedicating yourself to the process and constantly pushing beyond your limits. Someone else once said, "We've done so much, with so little, for so long. Now we can do anything with nothing." With an attitude like that, nothing will be impossible.

God is on your side and nothing is impossible with Him or you if you'll dig your heels in, throw your shoulders back, and never, ever give up. To achieve excellence, you must keep moving forward no matter what happens. Don't let anything stop you. Stand tall, work hard, dig deep and go after it. You can be excellent but first you must choose to be excellent. It all begins with a choice you make. Do you want the greatness excellence brings, or do you want to be average? When you choose excellence, you will hear your destiny calling you. Accept the challenge to reach your full potential and settle for nothing less. Stop making choices that don't make you better, that don't change you. Instead, make choices that will make you a champion, a legend, a person of excellence.

Get intense to the point that nothing will get in your way and stop you from fulfilling your dream. Yes, the spirit of excellence will take you to your destiny. It's not always about what you accomplish, it's about the effort you make. If you'll keep pressing forward and keep the effort going, excuses will be nonexistent. Excuses don't get results, determination and perseverance does. Be stronger than your excuses. The one life you've been given is too short to make excuses. Reach out and grab onto your dream and hold on. Regression is not always going backward; it's letting the opportunity outpace your courage. Don't let the ship of excellence sail past you. Grit your teeth and get on board. Push a little harder and you'll live the life of excellence like you've always dreamed.

| 3 |

"HOLD NOTHING BACK"

The pursuit of excellence should be one of the most exciting and enjoyable experiences of your life. The joy of working toward a goal is fundamental to your well-being. A person who has no goals to reach for and achieve is lost, aimlessly wandering without purpose. Ps. 29:18 says, "Where there is no vision, the people cast off restraint." But in Christ, we have the greatest goal to pursue, the goal of walking in excellence, the goal to be perfect like our Father in heaven is perfect (Matt. 5:48). Having clear goals to pursue always brings joy. But for a child of God, a goal is not joyful unless it has a sufficient challenge to it. For sure, real men and women love a challenge. God has given every person a high calling in Christ (Phil. 3:14). He expects each of us to live life according to the standards of heaven. That is a great challenge.

It is our duty to live up to that challenge. Jesus never compromises His standard of excellence. He is the same yesterday, today, and forever (Heb. 13:8). Goals can only bring us joy if we pursue them. This is why we must commit ourselves to the pursuit of excellence. We must press on toward the goal. Heb. 12:1,2 says, "Let us strip off every weight that slows us down. And let us run with endurance the race God has set before us. We do this by keeping our eyes on Jesus." Keep at it and never stop. 1 Cor. 15:58 says we are to "be steadfast, immovable, always abounding in the work of the Lord, knowing that your labor is not in vain." Pursuing excellence with all your heart leads to joy unspeakable and great satisfaction. It gives you something to live for, a reason to get up each and every morning.

Excellence and perfection are not the same thing. Perfection is the highest level of excellence. In other words, excellence is the journey you take to reach perfection. Excellence is doing your very best with what you now have. It's putting forth the highest quality of work and effort that you are capable of doing. It's when you hold nothing back. Most people don't think about excellence, but a real child of God thinks about it every second of their life. They are driven by the goal of becoming a person of excellence. The pursuit of excellence must be a continual endeavor. Why? Because times change. What is considered excellent today will be considered average tomorrow. The reward of pursuing excellence continually is you'll have constant and steady joy and pleasure. You'll have self-confidence believing you and God can do anything.

Don't put off your pursuit of excellence. Start right now. Whatever it is you are doing at this precise moment in time, perform at your highest level. Give total attention to the things you do. Moments of excellence turn into hours and days of excellence. Do this and the spirit of excellence will make you a perfect person. Check up on yourself and the things you do each and every day. Becoming a person of excellence will require continuous evaluation, the personal assessment of your efforts. Before you go to bed at night review everything you've done that day and consider what you could have done differently and with more excellence. Excellence will require time. You'll have to do less of some things so you can do other things better. Doing more can oftentimes be worse than doing less.

Any move toward excellence is a move away from mediocrity. Luke 2:52 says, "And Jesus increased in wisdom and stature, and in favor with God and man." Recognize that excellence is living a life of continuous change. Change is inevitable and is very important because it increases your rewards for being excellent. Change happens to everybody and a person of excellence will go "from glory to glory" (2 Cor. 3:18). The purpose of moving toward perfection is to experience the benefits of change. Excellence is impossible to hide. The servants of Boaz reported on the long hours of hard work Ruth had done in taking care of her mother-in-law (Ruth 2:11). Excellence doesn't require promotion, it promotes itself. It will be obvious to others when you perform at a high level. You can hide a flaw but you can't hide excellence.

At your work place give speedy attention to whatever your boss tells you to do. A person of excellence is diligent. They have an instant acceptance of any given assignment. There will be rewards for doing the best with what you have. Every step you take on your journey to perfection creates pleasure, an endless cycle of joy and happiness. Never lose sight of the eventual rewards of excellence. One of these rewards is you'll be accepted by those of character, leadership, and influence. When you become excellent in your thoughts, words, and actions, you will be pursued by others. Success and promotion will reach for you instead of you reaching for them. People will pay a high price for excellence. It is your responsibility to give it to them. Pursue excellence with all you've got and you will have a bright, bright future.

God has given every person the capacity to achieve excellence. Along the journey of life, He will usher in opportunities for you to fulfill your destiny to be great and to walk in excellence. The problem is most people don't get out of second gear. They've never stepped on the gas of the possibility and the potential to be all God called and created them to be. All men and women will one day regret things they have done but how many will regret things they did not do? God will forgive your sins but what cure is there for missed opportunities? What soothes the regret of not having done what you know you should have done with the energy and the possibilities God gifted you with to use for His glory? The biggest regret of all is to not maximize your life with excellence, to squander the best years of your existence by being average and mediocre.

God did not create you to simply exist, to take up space. He did not shape you in your mother's womb to just let life happen to you. Whatever will be, will be. God did not wake you up in the morning so you could sit idly by and watch other people pursue progress and excellence and achieve greatness in their lives. It is not your divine destiny to be idle, to be nothing more than a bystander in life. You were not created to sit on the dock at the lake all day wasting time. No, God has bigger plans for you than that. 1 Cor. 2:9 says, "Eye has not seen, nor ear heard, nor entered into the heart of men, the things God has prepared for those who love Him." Get on your knees and ask God for the spirit of excellence. Ask Him to maximize your possibilities, to live out your purpose, to help make this world a better place.

What distinguishes achievers from those who sit on the sidelines of life is achievers have a different spirit in them, a different mindset, a different attitude. The Bible is full of stories of ordinary people who overcame extraordinary obstacles to do great things for God because they had inside of them the spirit of excellence. There was something different in their heart and mind that allowed them to maximize all the possibilities God created for them, that allowed them to fulfill their destiny. One such man was Daniel. He was a man of prestige and had a renowned reputation, a man who rose to prominence in a foreign land because in him was an excellent spirit (Dan. 6:3). An excellent spirit will cause you to be distinguished in a crowd, to be successful in a hostile environment. It causes you to rise above everyone else and be noticed by others.

An excellent spirit will open doors for you that a college degree can't and money won't. It causes you to find favor with those who make important decisions. An excellent spirit will make you indispensable in any organization or company you work for. You won't be laid off when the other employees are shown the door. An excellent spirit will create opportunities for you that will pass other people by. You'll be the head and not the tail, above and not beneath (Deut. 28:13). Having an excellent spirit is what God requires of you to maximize the gift He has given you. It's what causes doors to open that would otherwise remain closed. Opportunities will be created and you'll boldly go where you've never gone before. It's the spirit of excellence that will launch you into greatness wherever you may be.

You will never maximize the opportunities in your life without an excellent spirit, when you expect more of yourself than what is required by others. An excellent spirit will compel you to set a standard that says there are some things that are not acceptable, those things that have your name on it. Dan. 6:3 says Daniel distinguished himself with an excellent spirit and you are to do the same. What Daniel had, nobody else had. Why? Because the spirit in him was very rare. Very few people have within them an excellent spirit. They let being average stop them from rising to the top, from being the best they could possibly be. These people will never experience the joy and satisfaction and fulfillment of living out the purpose and plan of God for the one life they've been given.

They're too busy thinking the world owes them something instead of them owing something to the world. This sense of entitlement stops them from seeking an excellent life. Daniel was an outsider who got promoted and those around him sought to take him down. Why? Because they felt entitled to the position Daniel was promoted to. They even tried to harm Daniel because entitlement is threatened by excellence. This is why some people will hate you even when you've done nothing wrong to them. We learn from Daniel that a spirit of excellence will take you farther than a sense of entitlement. Your attitude and the energy you put forth will take you higher than those around you. You can be an ordinary person with little or no education but with an excellent spirit and a hard work ethic you'll rise to the top of whatever it is God directs you to do.

Excellence is not what you do, it's who you are. You bring excellence to whatever you do, to everything you commit your hand to do. Why? Because excellence is who you are. You give your all to whatever endeavor you're undertaking because you know that mediocrity is the eternal enemy to excellence. To you, being average is not an option. Never will you do enough to just get by. To a person with a spirit of excellence, doing just enough is never enough. To them, being good enough is not good enough. Mediocrity is not in God's vocabulary. Doing just enough is not how God does things. He doesn't do anything half way. He does exceedingly abundantly above all that we ask or think (Eph. 3:20). There is a connection between your excellence and the glory God receives. Matt. 5:16, "Let your light shine before men that they may see your good works, and glorify your Father in heaven."

God cannot be glorified in mediocrity. You should do all you do with excellence so that others will know and declare that only God could have allowed you to do it. Does the work you do glorify God? Is He honored by others when they see the quality of the work you're doing? Do they see in you a spirit of excellence? Commit yourself to excellence. It is better to do one thing with excellence than to do many things average. It's not the quantity of what you do, it's the quality. Prioritize what you're committed to and bring excellence to it. Then let the work you do bring glory to God. Whatever your hand finds to do, do it with all your might (Eccl. 9:10). Now is the time to work with excellence, with care, energy, and purpose. The clock is ticking and now is the time to do the best you possibly can.

Excellence always separates itself from the normal standard. It's always improving. It's a commitment you make to constantly get better and better each and every day. Excellence is always an ongoing process. It's not something you do once and then do no more. Pursuing excellence is something you do all the days of your life. When you're a man of excellence whatever you do will be of the highest quality, a quality that always stands out. For something to be outstanding, it must stand out. Consider Prov. 22:29, "Do you see a man who excels in his work? He will stand before kings; He will not stand before unknown men." This tells us that excellence is observable. It is unavoidable that people will notice the excellent things you do. You may not see them watching you but, rest assured, they are.

This verse also tells us that excellence is related to some work you are doing. It makes sense that you can't be excellent if you're not doing anything. Also, excellence brings you out of the unknown. If unknown people are the only ones who see your work, then you are not yet a man of excellence. Excellence will raise you to the highest level. You'll be a person who will stand before kings. It will put you in the same circle of those who are of the highest rank and authority. In every field of life, excellence is a very desirable quality. Every person and every organization are looking for men and women of excellence. They'll spare no expense to find them. Promotion and the increased wages that go with it are all based on how excellent your work is. When you're excellent, you don't go looking for a job, it comes looking for you.

To fulfill your destiny, you must have a thirst and a hunger for excellence. Prov. 16:26 (NIV) says, "The appetite of laborers works for them; their hunger drives them on." The Message Bible says, "Appetite is an incentive to work; hunger makes you work all the harder." The work "hunger" is defined as 'the desire for something to meet our need.' For example, when you're hungry for food, you have a need for survival. Hunger is painful and it will drive you to work hard. People who are hungry never sit still and do nothing. Being hungry for excellence drives you forward. It pushes you beyond your normal limitations. Hunger causes you to excel in pursuing whatever it is you're hungry for. If you want to be excellent, you must be hungry for it. This desire will cause you to wake up in the morning vowing to do with excellence the best work you've ever done.

The work "appetite" is 'the capacity or the amount needed to satisfy us.' Hunger and appetite are not the same. Hunger deals with need while appetite deals with satisfaction. People who are average and mediocre will at times have a hunger for the things of God but their appetite is low. They get what they need but don't have the desire for more. Hunger tells you what you need but appetite determines how much you can have. When it comes to excellence, let us never be satisfied with what we have. Let us always desire more. In the world today the appetite for excellence is very low. People get satisfied way too soon. They're content being average. They don't have the desire or the drive for excellence. Never be satisfied with anything less than total and complete excellence. Always have a large appetite to be bigger and better than you are today.

| 4 |

"THE KEY TO PROMOTION"

I t is no secret that life in the world we live in can be hard and very confusing. People are running around like chickens with their heads cut off trying to make sense of it all. The Bible acknowledges this. Rom. 8:20 (TPT) says, "For against its will the universe itself has had to endure the empty futility resulting from the consequences of human sin." Solomon said in Eccl. 1:14, "I have seen all the works that are done under the sun; and indeed, all is vanity and grasping for the wind." Yet, in spite of all this, the people of God are challenged to find purpose and meaning in life. How? Jesus said, "Come to Me, all who are weary and burdened, and I will give you rest" (Matt. 11:28). He said, "Take My yoke upon you, and learn of Me; for I am meek and lowly in heart" (vs. 29). Throughout the Bible, God tells us that purpose in life is to learn and know who God is.

The more you learn of God and walk with Him, the more meaning life will have for you. By being close to God, you will learn the plan and purpose He has for your life. Daniel is a man

God used to model this for us. He found a way to find purpose and meaning in life even when life brings the most incredibly difficult circumstances. He purposed in his heart to live for God, refusing to be defiled by the worldly trappings around him. Every day he walked on the path God had for him. Daniel was a man who stood apart from everyone else because an excellent spirit was in him. Dan. 5:11 says in Daniel "is the Spirit of the Holy God." And because he refused to compromise his moral standards, Daniel not only survived this evil world, he thrived in it. He became a great leader in a dark, dark world.

Daniel was one of the greatest men who ever lived. There is nothing in the whole Bible said against him. He was truly a man with an excellent spirit. Excellence is the key to promotion, the key to seeing God's will come to pass in your life. You were created on purpose and you were created for a purpose. When you have an excellent spirit, it affects your character and your integrity. You'll understand that you are to be who God created you to be. Every child of God needs an excellent spirit. They need to be flawless like Daniel, a man who "was faithful, nor was there any error or fault found in him" (Dan. 6:4). Daniel was an extremely successful man in an extremely difficult time. He was a man of character with an excellent spirit and was used mightily by God.

We learn from Daniel that a person's character determines how far they will go in life. If your character is not right, rest assured, you are going nowhere. Nobody in the Bible better exemplifies a man of uncompromising character than Daniel. He was brimming with spirit and intelligence and completely outclassed everyone else. He was undeterred in his behavior believing it was better to obey God rather than man (Acts 5:29). This he did even at the risk of his own life. Daniel reminds us of Paul who declared in Acts 24:16, "I also do my best to maintain always a blameless conscience both before God and before men." Daniel's character and integrity was beyond question. He was faithful and trustworthy, and no spot or wrinkle or blemish was found in his life.

The life of Daniel teaches us how to pursue and develop an excellent spirit. The first thing we learn is Daniel had a willingness to stand out and be different from those around him. To be outstanding you have to stand out. You have to separate yourself from the rest of the world. It takes courage and sacrifice to be considered an outcast by everyone else. As a young lad he made the decision to serve God all the days of his life, and nothing was going to move him or get him to change his mind. Daniel was a man who stayed in the presence of God, and this brought forth growth in character. This growth comes from God and is vitally needed to operate in the spirit of excellence. He was a man of discipline. He purposed in his heart not to do wrong things. His devotion to God and his deep moral convictions were worth dying for.

Jesus said, "If you love Me, keep My commandments" (John 14;15). Paul told Timothy, "No man engaged in warfare entangles himself with worldly business" (2 Tim. 2:4). He had self-control and he had courage. He stood before Belshazzar the wicked king and preached him a sermon and warned him of judgment if he didn't repent of his sin. He lived for God and was a spiritual revolutionary in his day and time. He wouldn't let the Babylonian culture change him but he set out to change the Babylonian culture. Daniel exercised great integrity and received the respect and affection of the powerful rulers he served. His excellence gained him favor with the secular world. At the same time, his honesty and loyalty to his earthly masters never led him to compromise his faith and loyalty to the one true God.

Daniel is one of the best educated and most wise men in all the Bible. He was the prime minister under three emperors and three separate empires. His life glorified God as he advised kings for seventy years. His story reveals to all of us how marvelous a relationship a man can have with God if he chooses to walk in His ways. As children of God we are bound, like Daniel, to live in such a fashion so that others will have no doubt of the reality of the depth of our fellowship with Christ. Having an excellent spirit and strong character holds your life in balance. You won't be tossed to and fro by the winds of change and the storms of life. Like Daniel. your faith in God is strong. When Daniel came out of the lion's den Dan. 6:23 says, "No injury whatever was found on him, because he believed in his God."

Uncompromising character comes from the overflow of a faith-filled heart. Believe God and obey Him always and you will have an excellent spirit. Daniel had a long, eventful, and powerful life and his story begins when "Nebuchadnezzar king of Babylon came to Jerusalem and besieged it" (Dan. 1:1). Nebuchadnezzar was so strong and so powerful that he was feared throughout the known world. When he invaded a country victory for him was certain. His empire was powerful, impressive, and very massive. Because of that he wanted to recruit the most brilliant and educated men to serve under him. Dan. 1:3 says he brought "some of the children of Israel and some of the king's descendants and some of the nobles" back to Babylon with him.

Daniel was one of these young men. As a teenager he was put in chains and shackles and taken as a prisoner to the foreign land of Babylon which was 1700 miles away. The Babylonian empire was a highly advanced civilization. They were incredibly skilled and marvelous in architecture, astronomy, science, and mathematics. It was through Babylon that we know a circle has 360 degrees. They were able to track the planets in their orbits and they developed the calendar that we all use today. The Hanging Gardens of Babylon were one of the Seven Wonders of the ancient world. Legend has it that King Nebuchadnezzar had the gardens built as a gift to his wife Semiramis. The king wanted some young men who one day would be his advisers and counselors. He wanted to train them in all the ways of the Babylonian culture.

Dan. 1:4 says these men had natural gifts and abilities, had no natural defect, were quite handsome, and had a special aptitude to learn new things. They were well informed, quick to understand, and was highly qualified to serve in the king's palace. They had been carefully selected by Nebuchadnezzar's men. The standards in the king's palace were so high you had to be a person of high caliper in order to serve there. This gave them a higher realization of who they were. With a resume like that, a man could easily fall into pride. This is why Paul said in Phil. 2:3, "In lowliness of mind let each esteem others better than himself." All men need a sense of security about who they are in Christ. Paul said in 1 Cor. 15:10, "But by the grace of God I am what I am." He had an accurate assessment of who he was.

Of course, it matters not how great people think you are. What matters is are we really sufficient in the eyes of the King of kings and Lord of lords? Daniel had to learn a new language once he got to Babylon just as we do when we give our lives to Christ. We need to start speaking the things God wants to hear us say. Eph. 4:29 says, "Let no corrupt communication proceed out of your mouth, but what is good for necessary edification, that it might impart grace to the hearers." TPT, "And never let ugly or hateful words come from your mouth but instead let your words become beautiful gifts that encourage others." To be a man of excellence and serve in the king's palace you need an accurate assessment of who you are. You can't "think of yourself more highly than you ought to think" (Rom. 12:3).

At the same time, you must strive to reach the high standard God wants you to walk in. You must be strong in character with a spirit of excellence inside of you. Daniel began to step into his excellence right at the beginning of his exile in Babylon. He was considered the elite of the elite but walked in humility and didn't let arrogance take over his life. He didn't consider himself better than others because an excellent spirit was in him. Being humble goes along with having an accurate assessment of who you are. After all, 1 Cor. 1:28 says, "God has chosen the things which are not to bring to nothing the things that are." He chose what is insignificant to supersede what is prominent. MSG, "God deliberately chose men and women that the culture overlooks and exploits and abuses, chose the nobodies to expose the hollow pretensions of the somebodies."

The king instructed Ashpenaz, the chief of the court officials, to teach those chosen to serve in the king's palace the language and literature of the Babylonians (Dan. 1:4). He wanted to indoctrinate them with a new language, new books, new thoughts, and new literature. In other words, he wanted them to become as they were. The meaning of life grows dark when the light of heaven is diminished. It was the king's goal to take them as far away from their spiritual heritage as possible. Vs. 5, "The king assigned them a daily amount of food and wine from the king's table. They were to be trained   for three years, and after that they were to enter the king's service." He was going to force them to eat and drink things that went against their Hebrew dietary laws. His goal was to convert them into the Babylonian culture.

Vs. 6, "Now from among those of the sons of Judah were Daniel, Hananiah. Mishael, and Azariah." Together they would have their names changed from godly names to pagan names. The goal of the enemy is to change and confuse your identity, to call you something different from who and what God created you to be and to become. This is important because your name represents who you are. When an enemy wanted to take over your life, it was customary for them to change your name. In this case it would be a complete mockery of who God made them to be. In fact, it was done to obliterate the very nature of God on the inside of them. The enemy wants all men to not be known as children of God but something far less. The same thing that happened to Daniel and his three things is happening everywhere today.

The name "Daniel" means 'God is my Judge' and his name is changed to "Belteshazzar" which means 'Lady, protect the king.' Daniel is given a female name. This is eerie and very sinister because they're trying to change his gender. All the gender confusion in the world today happened also in the time of Daniel. The name "Hananiah" means 'The Lord is gracious' and his name was changed to "Shadrach" which means 'I am fearful of God.' That's a redefined spirituality and this same thing is happening in the world today. The enemy is doing everything he can to sow confusion in the church. The name "Mishael" means 'Who is as God?' and his name was changed to "Meshach" which means 'I am despised, contemptible, and humiliated.'

He believed there was no one like his God but the Babylonians tried to change what was an innocent set of emotions to depressed, anxious, fearful, and humiliated emotions. The enemy always tries to get involved with people's emotions. They can't sleep at night because the plan of the enemy is to bring fear and intimidation into their life. The name "Azarial" means 'The Lord is my help' and his name was changed to "Abed-Nego" which means 'Servant of Nebo,' another Babylonian false god. The name "Nebo" means 'one who speaks or prophesies.' They were no longer going to allow God to help him and direct his future, they were going to let the devil do it. By calling them names that glorified their false gods, the Babylonians were trying to remove from their memory their Hebrew names that glorified the one true, living God.

The lesson here is that when the culture shifts, you've got to know who you are. You were created by God, designed by God, and fashioned for God. And He has a plan for your life. God told Jeremiah, "Before I formed you in the womb I knew you, before you were born, I set you apart" (Jer. 1 :5). It's when you connect with God that you discover who you are. Always remember that this world is not your home. Yes, you're in the world but are not on the world (Jer. 17:16). You're no longer in the kingdom of darkness but in the kingdom of light. 2 Cor. 6:14 says, "Do not be yoked together with unbelievers. For what fellowship has righteousness with lawlessness? And what communion has light with darkness?" The excellence of your spirit binds you to Christ while at the same time separates you from the world. It's when you commit yourself to a godly standard of behavior.

 Charles Spurgeon said, "There must be a broad line of separation between the church and the world. It will be an evil day when that line is abolished." We are to be a light to the world without allowing the world to diminish our light. That is why 2 Cor. 6:17 says, "Come out from among them and be separate says the Lord." Is. 52:11 says, "Depart! Depart! Go out from there, touch no unclean thing; Go out from the midst of her, be clean you who bear the vessels of the Lord." Those with an excellent spirit dwell on the words of Rev. 18:4, "Come out of her, my people, so that you will not participate in her sins and receive her plagues." God has set you apart from the world and has called you unto Himself. Always practice the continual pursuit of holiness. Always remember who you are.

| 5 |

"NOT OF THIS WORLD"

Dan. 1:5 says the king of Babylon ordered Daniel and his friends to eat from the same menu he ate from. This included the best food and the finest wine. Daniel, however, was a man who had strong convictions. Dan.1:8 says, "But Daniel purposed in his heart that he would not defile himself with the portion of the king's delicacies." This is not about food. Daniel is purposing in his heart to keep his identity. He's living for God and is reminding these people he is not a Babylonian. He is in Babylon, but he is not a part of Babylon. He's a child of God and is not of this world. He is using food to tell his captors he is different than they are. A person with an excellent spirit doesn't want to be like everyone else. They don't want to fit in with the crowd. They want to be led by the Spirit of God and not by fleshly appetites.

Daniel didn't want to get drunk with the king's wine. He wanted a clear mind, to be sober-minded, to be in tune with God so he could know how to walk in wisdom. Eph. 5:18 (AMP) says, "Do not get drunk with wine, for that is wickedness, corruption, stupidity, but be filled with the Holy Spirit and constantly guided by Him." Daniel had a resolute heart and was unwavering in his convictions. He was saying, "I can't do that. That breaks my values, my doctrine. It goes against who I am." You must make up your mind what your core principles and values are. Then, with bold determination, you must never let anything take you from that. The world will always try to get you to compromise your moral standards that are based on the Word of God. Daniel stood his ground and fought for what he believed in.

When the culture shifts and goes in another direction, you must know what your beliefs are and where they came from. For those with an excellent spirit, they come from God Himself. To be successful in this world, you must have a made-up mind. You can't be "tossed to and fro and carried about with every wind of doctrine" (Eph. 4:14). Joshua was resolute when he said, "Choose for yourselves this day whom you will serve. But as for me and my house, we will serve the Lord" (Josh. 24:15). A strong, moral conviction is needed to live an excellent life. Always purpose in your heart to do what's right, to live the way God wants you to live. This will push you forward in life. You'll be forever determined to always obey God and not let mediocrity set in. A supernatural compulsion will drive you to do the right thing at all times.

Without hesitation, a person with an excellent spirit will follow the convictions in his heart. They won't go along with the people who care not what the will of God is. Daniel had a gracious determination. He was not rude or ill-mannered but kindly "requested of the chief of the eunuchs that he might not defile himself" (vs. 8). Most people purpose something in their heart and then demand they get what they want. Not Daniel. He was kind and considerate and showed reverence to those in authority. It takes faith to be this way. Real faith is so confident in the grace of God that what you purpose in your heart will be requested with ease even though you are strongly determined to get it. Dan. 1:9, "Now God had brought Daniel into the favor and good will of the chief of the eunuchs." This would not have happened had Daniel acted in a rude way.

Being excellent means to live completely without compromise, to have no deformity in your character, to be gracious to others no matter what it may cost you. One is reminded of Prov. 16:7 which says, "When a man's ways are pleasing to the Lord, he makes even his enemies to be at peace with him." Consider what happened to Joseph, "But the Lord was with Joseph and extended kindness to him, and gave him favor in the sight of the chief jailer" (Gen. 39:21). This favor shown Daniel is a beautiful example of the truth about God seen in Ps. 106:46, "He also made them objects of compassion in the presence of all their captors." Chares Spurgeon said, "In our very worst conditions our God has ways and means to find us helpers among those who have been our oppressors."

1 Kings 8:50 says, "Forgive your people who have sinned against You and make them objects of compassion before those who have taken them captive, that they may have compassion on them." When you have an excellent spirit God will start opening doors for you. Prov. 18:16 says, "A man's gift makes

room for him, and brings him before great men." This will happen if and when your gift is revealed with graciousness. Favor and good will come more because of being well-mannered than it does from having your particular gift. When you couple your gift with a spirit of graciousness you will discover God's favor in your life and in everything you set your hand to do. Great is an excellent spirit, a spirit that lives a lifestyle of being gracious. Col. 4:6 (AMP), "Let our speech at all times be gracious, pleasant, and winsome, seasoned as it were with salt."

The chief of the eunuchs responded to Daniel's gracious request, "I fear my lord the king, who has appointed your food and drink. For why should he see your faces looking worse than the young men who are your age? Then you would endanger my head before the king" (Dan. 1:10). This man was a palace servant, and he feared for his life. In the process of walking in excellence we must also take into account the feelings and the fears of other people. This man was afraid, and Daniel had to deal with it. He had such a confident expectation of how things would turn out that he listened carefully to this man's concerns. Daniel said to the man, "Please test your servants for ten days, and let them give us vegetables to eat and water to drink" (vs. 12).

"Then let our countenances be examined before you, and the countenances of the young men who eat the portion of the king's delicacies" (vs. 13). Then with words of faith he said, "And as you see fit, so deal with your servants." So the man consented with them in this matter and tested them ten days (vs. 13,14). We live in an evil world and today's culture will always test your faith. These tests are real, and you must be prepared for them when they do come. Charles Spurgeon said, "Fair weather may not outlast a single day. There is but a short space between one battle and another in this world." You need a solid foundation under you when the tests come and the storms of life blow. As the world gets darker and darker you must forever stand firm.

Consider 1 Cor. 16:13,14, "Be on your guard. Stand firm in the faith. Be courageous. Be strong. And do everything in love." The Message Bible says, "Keep your eyes open, hold tight to your convictions, give it all you've got, be resolute, and love without stopping." One way to stand firm is to stand in prayer. There is an evil spirit behind the thing you're standing firm against and your battle must always begin in the spiritual realm. Eph. 6:11,12 says, "Put on the full armor of God so that you can take your stand against the devil's schemes. For our struggle is not against flesh and blood." Paul says our struggle is "against the rulers, against the authorities, against the powers of this dark world and against the spiritual forces of evil in the heavenly realms" (vs. 12).

"Therefore put on the full armor of God, so that when the day of evil comes, you may be able to stand your ground, and after you have done everything, to stand" (vs. 13). Courage to stand firm in the midst of culture change comes through prayer. Go to your prayer closet and bind the spirit of the enemy that's trying to discourage you. Bind the spirit that's trying to put fear and intimidation in your heart. Stand firm in your convictions. And when you've done all you can to stand, keep on standing. In a dark world your light will shine brightly when you stand for the work of the Lord, the assignment He has given you to fulfill in His kingdom on the earth. Every man and woman has a part to play in the grand design of God. When you find your place and know what you're supposed to do, the courage and energy you need to stand firm will be there.

1 Cor. 15:58 says, "Be steadfast, immovable, always abounding in the work of the Lord, knowing that your labor is not in vain in the Lord." The NIV says, "Stand firm. Let nothing move you." Be stable in all you do and live your life with an unshakable confidence. God is truly on your side. MSG, "Stand your ground and don't hold back. Throw yourselves into the work of the Master, confident that nothing you do for Him is a waste of time or effort." Be steadfast in the work you do. Keep going forward and don't let up. Put your hand on the plow and don't take it off until your work is done. Always give yourself fully to the work of the Lord. Be constant, firm, resolute, not fickle or wavering, determined in purpose and in your loyalty to God.

To be steadfast means to be dedicated, dependable, enduring, established, immovable, loyal, single-minded, stable, unfaltering, unwavering, wholehearted. David declared in Ps. 108:1, "O God, my heart is steadfast; I will sing and give praise." Ps. 112:6 says the righteous "will not be afraid of evil tidings; His heart is steadfast, trusting in the Lord." When you take a stand, you must be immovable. You must keep your balance and remain unshaken when the rain comes down and the winds blow. Be like a boulder that can't be washed away or like a tree that can't get blown over. Let nothing move you away from your high moral standards. This is so important because when you take a stand, you're actually taking a stand for God. You're defending His honor and His glorious name.

People with an excellent spirit are firmly established in the faith and steadfast in their convictions to stand up for what is right in the eyes of God. Jesus said, "Everyone who acknowledges Me publicly here on earth, I will also acknowledge before My Father in heaven" (Matt. 10:32). MSG, "Stand up for Me against worldly opinion and I'll stand up for you before My Father in heaven." Put God first and He'll put you first. Take a stand and never be ashamed of the gospel of Christ. Stay focused on your assignment, keep praying and keep binding the spirit that's behind the problems in the world. When you take a stand, Jesus stands with you. Stephen took a stand and just before he was martyred said, "Look, I see the heavens opened and the Son of Man standing at the right hand of God" (Acts 7:56).

Jesus was sitting next to the Father (Col. 3:1) making intercession for the saints (Rom. 8:34). He then saw one of His servants take a stand and He stood up and took a stand also. When you take a stand, He'll never leave you alone. Deut. 31:8 says, "The Lord Himself goes before you and will be with you. He will never leave you nor forsake you. Do not be afraid." What are you afraid of? Take a stand knowing you are more than a conqueror (Rom. 8:37). Stand on the command of Jesus to take heart because He has overcome the world (John 16:33). Take a stand on the Word of God. Never bow down or give in or be persuaded to do anything contrary to God's will. Take a stand because no weapon formed against you will prosper (Is. 54:17). Never forget that God is on your side. Rom. 14:4 (AMP) says, "And he who serves the Master will stand because the Lord is able to make him stand."

Daniel is trusting God's faithfulness in this situation. He has an inner conviction that after ten days he'll look just as healthy as those who ate the king's food. With a gracious determination and a confident expectation Daniel told the man to put them to the test and then do to them as he saw fit. A man with a spirit of excellence has great confidence in the things he expects to happen. His faith in God is unwavering and his decisions and actions prove it. This type of faith and obedience comes from having a close heart-to-heart relationship with God. Doing this enables you to hear the words that are written on God's heart. Yes, faith comes by hearing the written Word of God, but it also comes from hearing the Word of God from the mouth of God, words He says to you personally.

Daniel's personal relationship with God is the reason he didn't want to partake of the king's food and wine. He thought he would be degraded and defiled if he did so. Daniel was in Babylon but was not part of the culture of Babylon. By refusing to eat the king's delicacies he was taking hold of God in a more powerful way. He did this because he wanted to be better equipped to serve not in the palace of the king of Babylon but in the palace of the King of kings and Lord of lords. In Daniel was an excellent spirit and for him there was no compromise in living a godly life. For him it was all or nothing. God's will was always first place in his life. Refusing to eat the king's food was the right thing to do. So confident was Daniel of what God was going to do he was willing to put his faith to the test.

Daniel talked to the chief of the eunuchs softly and gently because faith does not have to be loud. Confidence doesn't have to be constantly asserting itself for everyone to hear. Sometimes it's when people are shouting the loudest that you know they're the most insecure. Some people shout loud when their confidence is low and weak. The truth is, those who make the most noise have little or no content in the words they say. All their gibberish is nothing more than meaningless noise. Daniel was determined in his heart but gracious in his manner. He was confident in his expectation and therefore didn't have to be loud and boisterous. Men with an excellent spirit aren't after applause and acclamation. All they want is to one day hear God say, "Well done, good and faithful servant" (Matt. 25:23).

Daniel stayed back in the shadows, as it were, and God "who sees in secret will reward you openly" (Matt. 6:18). He knew a miracle would soon take place. Dan. 1:15, "And at the end of ten days their countenance appeared better and fatter in flesh than all the young men who ate the portion of the king's delicacies." Such a reversal of the laws of nutrition would require supernatural intervention, again a reflection of the fact that God "granted Daniel favor and compassion" (Dan. 1:9). It's worth noting that Daniel chose his battles wisely. He didn't object to being given a Babylonian name or to being trained in the language and learning of his captors. But when it came to the revealed law and will of God, Daniel was immovable. This was the first recorded exercise of faith on Daniel's part and it prepared him for greater tests to follow.

| 6 |

"ROYAL DREAMS"

Daniel 2 teaches us that those men and women who have an excellent spirit know the importance of pacing their lives in a way that will make them more effective and bring greater honor and glory to God. Dan. 2:1 says in the second year of King Nebuchadnezzar's reign he had a very disturbing dream "and his spirit was so troubled that his sleep left him." He is overly frustrated and very worried. He wants an interpretation of the dream and he wants it now. He is very impatient and no delay would be acceptable. With great urgency he called all the magicians, astrologers, sorcerers, and soothsayers and commanded them to tell him what his dream was along with its interpretation. The interpretation of royal dreams was an art in which they were all skilled. They even had manuals that listed various symbols that appeared in dreams along with their meaning.

There was just one problem. They had to know what the dream was. They said to the king, "Tell the dream to your servants, and we will declare the interpretation" (vs. 4). Those he called wanted the king to tell them the dream first and then they'd give the interpretation. But the king made it clear he wanted them to tell him what the dream was. Why is the king doing this? He wants to test the validity of those who stood before him. If they can tell him what the dream was, he can then trust their interpretation. By not divulging the dream itself to his would be interpreters he intends to make sure they're not leading him on by making up an interpretation of their own imagination (Vs. 9). He said, "My decision is firm. If you do not make known the dream to me, and its interpretation, you shall be cut in pieces, and your houses will be made an ash heap" (vs. 5).

It is interesting to note that Daniel was not brought in to see the king even though in all matters of wisdom and understanding he was ten times better than anyone else (Dan. 1:20). At some point in their lives all men have found themselves in the same situation. They know the solution to some problem, but no one bothered to ask them to get involved. God's ways are not our ways (Is. 55:8) and sometimes He uses a strategy to get us to learn valuable lessons   through the pain of being overlooked. Not only is Daniel being overlooked but he's about to lose his life because of everyone else's incompetence and their inability to tell the king what the dream was. The king is told, "It is a difficult thing that the king requires, and there is no other who can tell it to the king, except the gods, whose dwelling is not with flesh" (vs. 11).

Never before had an interpretation of a dream been required to reconstruct the dream itself. Not even Joseph in Egypt was told to tell Pharaoh what his dream was. This admission reflects the inability of occult powers to give divine revelation. It shows that they've been deceiving the king all along and are deserving of the death sentence. "For this reason the king was angry and very furious" (vs. 12). A deep disturbance overcame him and he "gave a command to destroy all the wise men of Babylon." The king's anxiety was caused by his desire to know the meaning of the dream. He was the king and had what all men desire yet he lacked one thing. Peace of mind. The king is in a mental state of distress and worry. "So the decree went out and they began killing the wise men; and they sought Daniel and his companions to kill them" (vs. 13).

It has been said that the true character of a person is revealed in a time of crisis. For sure, Daniel faced a great crisis when the royal executioner stood at his door. God had prepared and equipped Daniel for such a time as this. His response is an example of how all people with an excellent spirit should react to a crisis. Dan. 1:14 says, "Then with counsel and wisdom Daniel answered Arioch, the captain of the king's guard, who had gone out to kill the wise men of Babylon." Daniel spoke with discretion and discernment. He was a young man but wise in the ways of God. He did not panic. He did not overreact. He did not become paralyzed with fear. Daniel could have easily become frightened, but his response reflected the truth of Prov. 29:25, "The fear of man brings a snare, but he who trusts in the Lord will be exalted."

Daniel is shown to be a man of great character who has learned how to trust God. He recognized that a humanly impossible situation can only be resolved by divine intervention. Daniel knew that our obstacles are God's opportunities to show Himself great and mighty on our behalf. His response was based on God's provision of favor and compassion. Daniel was tactful and wise in his approach to the very man who had been assigned to take his life. Prov. 15:1 says, "A gentle answer turns away wrath." Daniel wasn't rude or overbearing or argumentative. Col. 4:5,6 says, "Conduct yourselves with wisdom toward outsiders, making the most of the opportunity. Let your speech always be with grace, as though seasoned with salt, so that you will know how you should respond to each person."

Daniel is completely dominated in his soul by his complete faith in God. He has stability, he has strength, he has poise under pressure. He is cool, calm, and collected. "He answered and said to Arioch the king's captain, 'Why is the decree from the king so urgent?' Then Arioch made the decision known to Daniel" (vs. 15). It is a miracle in itself that Arioch took time to listen to Daniel. Most rough men would have cared less if their intended victims knew why they were being killed. Daniel asked what was going on and then listened so he could understand the whole picture. Prov. 18:13, "If one gives an answer before he hears, it is his folly and shame." It is vital to get all the facts about a situation before jumping in to share your opinion. Many arguments could be avoided by first asking simple, neutral questions.

Doing this can give you a more clear understanding of the whole picture rather than acting foolishly based on assumptions that may turn out to be false. Daniel asked why there was an urgency in this matter and it can be assumed that Arioch told him about the king's dream and his frustration that it was not revealed and interpreted. In faith Daniel made a bold move. Vs. 16 says, "So Daniel went in and asked the king to give him time, that he might tell the king the interpretation." Here is Daniel standing in the very presence of the man who angrily ordered his death. This is yet another manifestation of God granting him favor and compassion in the presence of his enemies. Daniel is most persuasive with the king. He asks for time to seek an interpretation of the dream when previously the king accused the wise men of stall tactics (vs.8).

The reason for Daniel's boldness was that the Holy Spirit was active in his life at this time of great crisis. It's what prompted him to seek an audience with the king. In Acts 4:31 we see that after praying the saints "were all filled with the Holy Spirit, and they spoke the Word of God with boldness." Daniel was a lamb among a pack of wolves and still he reverently asked the king to give him the one thing he vehemently refused to give anyone else. Time. Time is a valuable commodity in a fast-paced world where everyone has the need for speed. Nobody wants to pace themselves anymore not realizing that good things come to those who wait. They say patience is a virtue. When things don't go according to plan, patience gives us the strength and determination to remain optimistic.

In a busy, frantic, and demanding world, patience is a valuable asset. It keeps people focused on long-term goals and less frustrated by temporary setbacks. Patience cultivates sound judgment. In a world that feels rushed and demanding, the ability to pace yourself and tolerate delays empowers us to make clear-headed decisions. Daniel's boldness reveals a lot about his confidence and his knowledge of God. He knows God hears the cries of our heart and delivers those who trust in Him. Daniel's boldness and his excellent spirit and calm assurance helped him to impress the king who then granted his request for time which he refused to give his other advisors. This is another miracle considering how brutally ferocious the king had been, how savage and severely vicious he was when he ordered the deaths of all the wise men.

Men with an excellent spirit work smarter, not faster. They know there is enough time in the day to do what God has told them to do. God always gives you enough time to fulfill your calling. Men put too much pressure on themselves by thinking they have to accomplish their assignment sooner than they have to. Stop acting as if you're going to die tomorrow. You don't have to get everything done today. Slow down and pace yourself. Ps. 31:15 says, "My times are in Your hand." Patience will help you avoid acting out of frustration and anger thus preventing you from making hasty choices that could have negative consequences. Daniel asked, "What's the urgency?" He knew patience helps you navigate challenges with a level head. It fosters resilience and helps you handle adversity with grace.

It takes work and effort to pace yourself in a fast world. Many people died because Nebuchadnezzar did not have the patience to wait for the answer he wanted. People who pressure themselves to do things in a hurry accomplish less than those who take their time to do things in a proper and timely manner. Be aware that this is not a recipe for laziness. Don't be like those who put off until tomorrow the things they should be doing today. Don't live hoping someone will come along and do the work for you. No, the responsibility to do the work is yours. Just pace yourself and do it right. Rest assured, God will give you the time to do the things that need to be done. He'll give you the space you need. Reschedule your life and watch what happens.

In the midst of all this you must recognize the sovereignty of God, that He has the right and the power to do all that He decides to do. Job 42:2 says, "I know that You can do everything, and that no purpose of Yours can be withheld from You." MSG, "Nothing and no one can upset Your plans." This being true, it is therefore foolish to take the management of your time out of His very capable hands and put it into your own hands. You must give God permission to manage your time on a minute-by-minute basis. After all, it is He who rules over the affairs of men (Dan. 4:17). It is your responsibility to make sure that everything that happens in your life lines up with the will of God. Let Him tell you what to do and when to do it.

Time management is so important because of the brevity of our lives. James 4:14 says, "You are a mist that appears for a little while and then vanishes." Indeed, our time on earth is fleeting. To live as God would have us live, we must make the best use of our allotted time here which is very small when compared to eternity. Eccl. 3:11 says God has put eternity in our hearts. Knowing that we will have to give an account to Him who gives us time should motivate us to use it well. Use your time carefully. Eph. 5:16,17 (NLT) says, "Make the most of every opportunity in these evil days. Don't act thoughtlessly but understand what the Lord wants you to do." TPT, "Take full advantage of every day as you spend your life for His purposes. And don't live foolishly for then you will have discernment to fully understand God's will."

Not only did God give us life and life more abundantly (John 10:10), He also gave us time to enjoy it. Thankfully, He also gave us guidelines on how to spend it. Because life is so precious, we must make the most of every moment we are here. When you wake up each morning ask God how He wants you to manage your day. Ps. 90:12 says, "Teach us to number our days, that we may gain a heart of wisdom." Every day live for the glory of God and to be a witness to His goodness and saving grace. Live daily with eternity in your heart and mind. Eccl. 3:11 says, "Yet God has made everything beautiful for its own time. He has planted eternity in the human heart." When you know what God wants you to do, make plans to do it in a timely manner and not at the last minute for it might never get done.

Prov. 6:4 (NLT) says, "Don't put it off; do it now! Don't rest until you do." Procrastination is the enemy of success. James 4:17, "It is sin to know what you ought to do and then not do it." Also, don't take on more than you can handle. Don't over commit yourself. Learn to say "no" to something that sounds good if it interferes with your other obligations. Pace yourself and don't become a workaholic. Take time to get the rest you need. Matt. 11:28 says, "Come to Me, all you who are weary and burdened, and I will give you rest." The Bible warns against laziness so pray for wisdom in not becoming a workaholic but also not sleeping away the days neglecting your responsibilities. Use your time wisely because God wants you to live a stress-free life while at the same time fulfilling your obligations without worry and frustration.

Knowing that time is quickly dwindling away should compel you to make better use of your time. You must pace yourself to avoid losing focus on what God wants you to do. Time is precious and very valuable, and you must work diligently to make the most use of the time you've been given. To waste your time is to waste your life. The Parable of the Talents (Matt. 25:14-30) illustrates the tragedy of wasted time and opportunity as well as the importance of laboring faithfully until the Lord comes. Spend quality time with God for He is the one who entrusted you with this time on the earth and He is the one who decides how you should spend it. Time belongs to God so ask for His wisdom in how best to use it. When divine direction comes you must go forward with boldness and confidence.

Make a concentrated effort to consider how you spend your time. Consider the things God deems important and valuable. Consider what He has called you to do specifically. Make a list of your priorities and responsibilities and ask God to direct you regarding any changes that need to be made so you can make the most of your time. The Bible says you need to place your focus and spend your time on that which is eternal as opposed to the fleeting pleasures of this passing world. Pace yourself and move forward with diligence and divine purpose as you "press toward the goal for the prize of the upward call of God in Christ Jesus (Phil. 3:14). Time spent doing the things God tells you to do is time well spent because you will bear eternal fruit. Live as if each minute counts because it really does.

| 7 |

"SACRED DELIGHT"

The Bible makes it clear that Daniel had an excellent spirit. As men and women of God we must take hold of that same spirit of excellence and have it manifested in our life. We need to tap into the same calmness that Daniel had. He faced adversity with a spirit of serenity. He knew his walk with God was not a pressurized walk. Consider James 3:13, "Who is wise and understanding among you? Let him show by good conduct that his works are done in the meekness of wisdom." TPT, "If you consider yourself to be wise and one who understands the ways of God, advertise it with a beautiful, fruitful life guided by wisdom's gentleness." Wisdom always has meekness attached to it. Vs. 17 (TPT) says, "The wisdom from above is always pure, filled with peace, considerate and teachable."

"It is filled with love and never displays prejudice or hypocrisy in any form." MSG, "It is gentle and reasonable, overflowing with mercy and blessings." Daniel had a wisdom that was pure, peaceful, and gentle. He had a confidence in his heart that God will protect him and his friends no matter what happens. Along with an excellent spirit Daniel had wisdom that was "full of mercy and food fruits, without partiality and without hypocrisy" (vs. 17). Vs. 18 (TPT) says wisdom "always bears the beautiful harvest of righteousness! Good seeds of wisdom's fruit will be planted with peaceful acts by those who cherish making peace." There was no envy and strife in Daniel's demeanor. There was no confusion and he didn't open the door to the attacks of the enemy. He had peace in the midst of the storm.

Excellence is not about running around in circles nor is it about idleness. It's about tapping into the heart of God and discovering His timing on when to do things. Is. 40:31, "But they that wait upon the Lord shall renew their strength; They shall mount up with wings as eagles; They shall run and not be weary; They shall walk and not faint." What's more, those with an excellent spirit know when they're meant to fly, when they're meant to run, and when they're meant to walk. No matter how old or young you are, there will be times when God wants you to fly high in the heavenlies on the wind currents of the Holy Spirit. At other times, like with the situation facing Daniel, the king's business will require hustle where you'll have to run and do things quickly.

And then there are times when flying and running are not appropriate, times when you need to pace yourself and slow down, to walk quietly as you wait on the Lord. Not only when you wait on the Lord will you receive strength to fly, run, and walk, you'll also receive the wisdom to know what to do and when to do it. The second chapter of Daniel begins with the king of Babylon being in a troubled and distressed frame of mind. This opened a door of opportunity that Daniel walked through. The king had a very disturbing dream and wanted to know its interpretation. With wisdom and discretion Daniel calmly asked the king for time and then he'd give him the interpretation. He did not panic even though his life is clearly on the line. He is still a teenager or possibly early 20's but he is a lad who knows his God.

Prov. 3:25,26 says, "Do not be afraid of sudden fear nor of the onslaught of the wicked when it comes. For the Lord God will be your confidence and keep your foot from being caught." World War II Major and evangelist W. Ian Thomas said, "It is the presence of the Lord Jesus that allows a man to be gloriously detached from the pressure of circumstance." Someone once asked Albert Einstein's wife if she understood the theory of relativity. She replied that she didn't but Albert did and he could be trusted. How much more should we trust God in times of trial and testing? We may not know what's going on but God does and surely He can be trusted. Trust God and "you'll take afternoon naps without a worry, you'll enjoy a good night's sleep. There will be no need to panic over alarms or surprises" (Prov. 3:24,25 MSG).

English Puritan preacher and author Thomas Watson said in the 17th century, "God is to be trusted when His providences seem to run contrary to His promises." What's the first thing Daniel did when he left the presence of the king? Vs. 17, "Then Daniel went to his house and made the decision known to Hananiah, Mishael, and Azariah, his companions." In other words, he called a prayer meeting with those closest to him. He didn't consult the magic books of Babylon; he consulted the Most High God of the universe. "He urged them to plead for mercy from the God of heaven concerning this mystery, so that he and his friends might not be executed with the rest of the wise men of Babylon" (vs. 18). Without hesitation Daniel went into action and began to pray with his friends. Likewise, make sure you have other believers around you that you can ask to pray in times of trial.

This is the first recorded prayer meeting in the Bible. They practiced Matt. 7:7 before it was even written, "Ask, and it shall be given you; seek, and you will find; knock, and it will be given to you." Praying together is extremely powerful and is always more effective than panic. Charles Spurgeon said his success in the pulpit came from saints in a lower room interceding with God. In Acts 4:24 we see the saints praying together lifting "their voices to God with one accord." Daniel and his friends also prayed with one accord, with the same mind and purpose. Daniel and his companions know that God is "compassionate and gracious" (Ex. 34:6). They also know from the story of Joseph that God alone reveals the meaning of dreams (Gen. 40:5). Because of Joseph's experience in Egypt, Daniel and his friends have good cause to believe in the power of their petition for mercy in their prayer to God.

The wise men of Babylon could not communicate with their gods but Daniel and his friends knew they could get in touch with the living God of Israel. For this reason, they did not panic but instead prayed with faith and confidence. They prayed for mercy and compassion being sure they would receive it. Pastor Jon Courson said, "Nebuchadnezzar took his problems to bed. Daniel took his to God and what a difference that makes." Also, take note that Solomon had prayed 300 years earlier for God to make His chosen people "objects of compassion before those who have taken them captive" (1 Kings 8:50). Could the compassion Daniel and his friends are experiencing be in part an answer to Solomon's ancient prayer? Indeed, it could which shows the timeless significance of our prayers to God.

Daniel was a righteous man who feared God. Ps. 145:19 says, "He will fulfill the desires of those who fear Him; He will also hear their cry and save them." God likes it when His children cry out to Him in prayer. Ps. 141:2, "May my prayer be counted as incense before You; The lifting of my hands as the evening offering." What is prayer? In simple terms, it's talking to God. It is the communication of the human soul with the God who created the human soul. Prayer can be audible or silent, private or public, and it must be offered in faith (James 1:6), in the name of the Lord Jesus (John 16:23), and in the power of the Holy Spirit (Rom. 8:26). The wicked have no desire to pray (Ps. 10:4) but the children of God have a natural desire to pray (Luke 11:1) for it draws them closer to God (Ps. 73:28).

Charles Spurgeon said, "Prayer gives a channel to the pent-up sorrows of the soul, they flow away, and in their stead streams of sacred delight pour into the heart." How often should we pray? The biblical answer is to "pray without ceasing" (1 Thess. 5:17). All men should have a conversation going on with God all day long. Like Daniel, David also prayed without ceasing. He said in Ps. 55:17, "Evening and morning and at noon I will pray, and cry aloud, and He shall hear my voice." To begin, continue, and end the day in the presence of God is supreme wisdom. Day and night the enemy will try to take you down. You fight him off with continuous prayer. David prayed with the confidence that he would prevail over his enemies. He had no doubt that his prayers would be heard. He prayed as if they were already answered.

Regular, daily prayer takes discipline and continual effort. Some people go through the day without speaking to God even once. This should not be. Prayer is a vital part of a believer's role as one who is beloved of God the Father. It's an expression of your total dependence on Him and Him alone. Paul said in Eph. 6:18 (NLT), "Pray in the Spirit at all times and on every occasion. Stay alert and be persistent in your prayers for all believers everywhere." Charles Spurgeon said, "Prayer must not be our random work but our daily business, our habit, and our vocation. We must be immersed in prayer and so pray without ceasing." Prayer to God should be made persistently (Luke 18:1), with thanksgiving (Phil. 4:6), in faith (James 1:5), within the will of God (Matt. 6:10), and for the glory of God (John 14:13).

1 Peter 3:12 says, "For the eyes of the Lord are on the righteous, and His ears are open to their prayers." The MSG says God is "listening and responding well to what He's asked." God observes the righteous with approval and tender consideration. They are dear to Him and His ears are open to their cry. He is

not slow to answer the requests of His children. The passionate prayers of God's righteous children can accomplish much. The barren Hannah's steadfast and humble prayers resulted in the birth of the prophet Samuel (1 Sam. 1:20). Prayer saved the righteous Daniel from the lion's den (Dan. 6:11) and in the New Testament the apostle Paul's prayers even caused the earth to shake (Acts 16:26). The same God who made the sun stand still because of the prayer of Joshua (Josh. 10:13) invites us to come boldly to the throne of grace where we'll find help in our time of need (Heb. 4:16).

Daniel and his friends prayed and then a miracle happened. Dan. 2:19 says, "Then the secret was revealed to Daniel in a night vision. So Daniel blessed the God of heaven." The secret counsels of God remain hidden from the ungodly - to them they are a mystery - but are revealed to the godly and are understood by them. We do not know whether Daniel kept praying until he received an answer or whether he was able to rest and sleep without yet getting the answer. Either way, Daniel showed great faith in a faithful God. Evg. George Muller said in the 19th century, "If our circumstances find us in God, we shall find God in our circumstances." What happened next? Daniel immediately expresses his gratitude to God above. He didn't run to Arioch or to the king but got on his knees and worshiped God.

One can only imagine how much joy and amazement was in his heart toward the Lord who had revealed this great mystery and saved him from a certain death. David Guzik said, "Our level of faith is often indicated by how long it takes us to start praising

God. Greater faith is able to praise God when the promise and given and received." The Hebrew word for "blessed" is "barik" and conveys the idea of offering worship and praise while on one's knees. It also means 'to give honor to or to speak good of.' Daniel then proceeded to speak many good words about God, specifically declaring seven things that give Him glory. He was giving credit to the one to whom all credit belongs. Those with the spirit of excellence do the same thing. They're like the cleansed leper who returned to give thanks to Jesus and not like the nine who never returned (Luke 17:12-19).

The first thing Daniel says is "Blessed be the name of God forever and ever, for wisdom and might are His (Dan. 2:20). For sure, "the name of the Lord is a strong tower" (Prov. 18:10). David also knew this to be true for he said in Ps. 20:7, "Some trust in chariots, and some in horses; But we will remember the name of the Lord our God." God's name speaks of who He is everything He stands for. It encompasses all His attributes and qualities. It represents His self-revelation, an expression of His revealed character. Those with an excellent spirit can confidently and safely take refuge in God's name. In His name there is as assurance of security and well-being. To be protected by God's name is to be protected by the one who is sovereign, holy, all-knowing, wise, compassionate, full of grace and full of mercy.

Jesus prayed in John 17:11, "Holy Father, each one that You have given Me, keep them in Your name so that they will be united as one, even as we are one." The name of God is so holy that the ancient Jews never pronounced it in public. When they came to it in reading, they would pass over it in reverent silence. Men and women of excellence honor God's name in their heart and in their life. Jesus taught us to pray, "Our Father in heaven, hallowed be Your name" (Matt. 6:9). The Greek word for "hallowed" is "hagios" and means 'set apart, holy, sanctified, consecrated.' When you pray you acknowledge that God is holy and unlike any other. All believers are to hold His name in deep reverence. By doing so they honor, glorify, and exalt Him for His name speaks of His person and character.

Jesus is teaching the citizens of His kingdom to recognize the greatness of God's name and to always give Him the honor and glory He so richly deserves. The request "hallowed be Thy name" comes first in the Lord's Prayer. Right away Jesus removes the focus from us and turns our attention to God. In other words, it's all about Him. Jesus taught us to begin our prayers by recognizing the God to whom we pray. He is holy and worthy of all honor and praise. He wants us to see how glorious the Father is. Yes, God's name is above every name (Phil. 2:9). Let God's name be reverenced above all other names. Let His name be given a position which is absolutely unique. The phrase "hallowed be Thy name" literally means, "Enable us to give to Thee the unique place which Thy nature and character deserve and demand."

Daniel knew the value of God's name. Ps. 9:10 says, "And those who know Your name will put their trust in You, for You, O Lord, have not forsaken those who seek You." Those with an excellent spirit speak of God with great reverence. They never profane God's name with their mouths and never do they take

His name in vain. We hallow His name by living a life that displays that He is our Father. Daily we dedicate ourselves to doing and saying things that give reverence to all that He is. People of excellence live fully for the glory of God. They hallow His name by surrendering to the call on their lives. They say, "He must increase and I must decrease" (John 3:30). Pastor Red Stedman said, "May the whole of my life be a source of delight to You and may it be an honor to the name I bear. Hallowed be Your name."

| 8 |

"A NEW THING"

Nebuchadnezzar had a dream in which he saw a great and impressive statue that was smashed by a stone that became a great mountain that filled the earth. God revealed to Daniel that this statue represented four successive kingdoms, beginning with the current Babylonian kingdom and ending with the everlasting kingdom of the God of heaven. When God gave Daniel the interpretation of the dream it launched Daniel's career as a political leader, trusted adviser, and well-known prophet. Daniel was indeed a unique individual. In him was an excellent spirit and in the midst of despair and chaos there was hope in his heart. The disparity of the world around him and the craziness of the Babylonian culture did not deter him from believing God was right there in the middle of it all.

When God answered his prayer Daniel proclaimed, "Praise be to the name of God forever and ever. He changes the times and the seasons. He removes kings and raises up kings" (Dan. 2:20,21). He is declaring that God is actively involved in ways they could not see. He goes on to say, "He gives wisdom to the wise and knowledge to those who have understanding. He reveals deep and secret things; He knows what is in the darkness, and light dwells with Him" (vs. 21, 22). God sees the darkness and causes His people to be light in the midst of it. "I thank You and praise You, O God of my fathers; You have given me wisdom and might and have now made known to me what was asked of You" (vs. 23). What Daniel is saying is that the flow of human history is not determined by earthly kings and rulers but by the sovereign hand of God.

History is literally "His story" and He controls the flow of history either in an active or permissive manner. The NLT says, "He controls the course of world events." Daniel correctly perceived God as being more powerful than any earthly king. He is in control and it is He who determines who occupies earthly thrones (Rom. 13:1). Ps. 75:6,7 says, "For exaltation comes neither from the east nor from the west nor from the south, but God is the Judge. He puts down one, and exalts another." This tells us that God has the ability to control what goes on in the earth. Never forget that He has the ultimate   authority and it is His plan that will be done. At the same time, He is looking for us to work with Him. He seeks men and women with a spirit of excellence whom He can partner with to accomplish His will.

As we cooperate with Him, we can participate in the manifestation of His plan and help bring it to pass. To do that we must understand the times and seasons of God. Man measures his existence on planet earth in quantities of time known as minutes, hours, days, weeks, and years. God, on the other hand, measures time in seasons. Seasons represent different times in our human existence and they are necessary and essential to our life experience. Never fear the changing of the times. Seasons were created and directed by God. Solomon, the wise king and philosopher, said in Eccl. 3:1, "To everything there is a season, a time for every purpose under heaven." God made "every nation of men to dwell on the earth and has determined their preappointed times and the boundaries of their habitation" (Acts 17:26).

God is the source of our life, breath, and everything we need. It is He who determines where we reside, and it is through Him that "we live and move and have our being" (Acts 17:28). Most things don't happen instantly in the life of a person who has an excellent spirit. Spiritual maturity is developed and not received and this takes time. Any farmer will testify that in order to receive a bountiful crop from his efforts the seeds he sows must go through a variety of seasons. First there is the planting season followed by a watering season, a growth and development season, and finally there is the harvest season. All these seasons have different characteristics and features that surround the different stages of growth that the plant is in.

A plant doesn't mature instantly. Therefore, it is vitally important for that plant to go through each and every season in its growth and development. Some people think if their prayers are not answered immediately that something is wrong. This is not always true for there is a process of time involved in walking in the things of God. We inherit the promises of God through faith and patience (Heb. 6:12). Patience is developed by remaining strong and steadfast in the seasons of tests and trials (James 1:2-4). With God a delay is not a denial. When He wants to make a mushroom, He does it overnight. When He wants to make a giant oak tree, He takes hundreds of years. Solomon tells us that if we cooperate with God's purposes and timing that life will not be meaningless. Eccl. 3:11 says, "He has made everything beautiful in its time."

God ordains the seasons we are in and throughout our life, from before our birth to the day of our passing, He is accomplishing His divine purposes. Every event in your life has a season, an appropriate time not produced randomly but in a manner that is in line with God's plan for your life. Know also that a season has a beginning and an end. In nature there are four seasons we go through each year. There is spring, summer, fall, and winter. Each one has particular features and different characteristics from the others but it is important that we go through each and every season. Likewise, it is also important that we experience all of God's seasons and go through different things so that we can grow and develop in the things of God.

Pause and consider a moment the seasons God has ordained for men to walk through. Without much thought you'll easily see some of their purposes. Spring is the time of new beginnings, exciting opportunities, and anticipation for the future. Spring is about potential, promise, planning, and possibilities. Summer is a time of growth when the seeds we planted mature into full grown plants. Summer is a season of work when we invest the time and effort required to be good at what we do. Working hard produces a bountiful harvest in the fall season. It's when all the blood, sweat, and tears you have shed begin to pay off rewarding you for all your hard labor. Winter is the season of winding down, withdrawal, retreat, and closure. It represents a period of rest, restoration, and reflection on all you've done.

Seasons are not permanent and the season you are now in will soon pass. Once winter passes, another spring is at your doorstep. The key is to keep moving forward. Is. 43:18,19 says, "Forget the former things; do not dwell on the past. See, I am doing a new thing! Now it shall spring forth." People of excellence embrace whatever season they may be in. They know that various seasons are a part of God's plan and purpose for their life. No matter what season you find yourself in, it is vitally important to fully engage with it and embrace it with all you've got. All too often people want to skip a season. They want to jump straight from the planting season to the harvest season without doing all the work in the summer season.

Doing this disrupts the entire process. The way you handle one season profoundly impacts how you experience all the other seasons that follow. Embracing each season in its proper sequence and faithfully fulfilling the responsibility it calls for is crucial for a fruitful and fulfilling life. On the other hand, staying in a season too long can also have adverse effects. Life is a journey and we must forever be going forward. Clinging to a season too long can hinder your growth and prevent you from fully embracing the opportunities that the next season will bring you. The way to live the most fulfilling life possible is to recognize when it's time to let go thus allowing yourself to gracefully enter the new season that awaits you.

Seasons are God-ordained and purposeful so enjoy the season you are in. Take comfort knowing that He is working all things for His good will and purpose (Rom. 8:28). God wants every person to know that even in the middle of a trial, in the midst of adversity and despair, that He's at work on the earth and He is in control. This is why Daniel said that God "removes kings and raises up kings" (vs. 21). The king's dream clearly shows kingdoms rising and falling in succession just as God ordained. God alone determines when events are to take place and how long each phase in history lasts. God indeed has providence over the history of mankind. People of excellence know things don't just happen to those who love God. No, they're planned with foresight and timely care. He is the potter molding and shaping their lives according to His will.

Job spoke of this when he declared, "I know that You can do all things, and that no purpose of Yours can be withheld from You" (Job 42:2). This teaches us that there is no such thing as luck, chance, fate, or coincidence. God rules the universe and is too powerful and sovereign to be lucky. God orders history through His removal and establishment of world rulers. This is what Nebuchadnezzar's dream was all about. It tells us there are no self-made dictators. Yes, some kings are evil and do bad things. God, however, can bring good out of anything even when flawed rulers are involved. He is truly the real power behind the throne. For example, King Ahasuerus was king over the Persian empire and God used some unusual events to replace his wife with Esther, a Jewish girl who later saved His people from annihilation.

God is the supreme, all-powerful ruler of the universe. The MSG says, "He knows all, does all." Daniel said in vs. 22, "It is He who reveals the deep and secret things." Theologian Albert Barnes said the secret things is "knowledge which lies beyond any natural compass of the human powers, and in which a supernatural influence is needed." There is no way for man to know about the future except through a revelation from God. Job 12:22 says, "He reveals mysteries from the darkness, and brings the deep darkness into light." Amos 3:7, "Surely the Lord God does nothing unless He reveals His secret to His servants the prophets." Daniel was a vessel of honor "prepared for every good work" (2 Tim. 2:21). Daniel was used mightily of God. 2 Peter 1:21 says, "For no prophesy was ever made by an act of human will, but holy men spoke as they were moved by the Holy Spirit."

Daniel praised God for giving him wisdom and power and the interpretation of the king's dream (vs. 23). When he did so he called God the "God of my fathers." This name emphasizes God's covenant faithfulness and is rooted in the covenant He established with Abraham, Isaac, and Jacob (Ex. 2:24). Daniel understood that despite being a captive in a foreign land and all other outward circumstances, God was still bound by His promise to the forefathers. Daniel praised God for His power and might knowing He is in command of all things. He knew God is mightier than a mighty king like Nebuchadnezzar. He also praised God for His communication with man. All of

God's power and might would have been of little help to Daniel if He had stayed silent and not revealed His great knowledge.

We can endure the seasons and culture changes we go through if we have confidence knowing that God has the whole world in His hands. He is always at work and people of faith know that. This doesn't mean you relax and do nothing. On the contrary, you fight the good fight of faith even harder. Work hard and let God use you to speak life and clarity into the confusion of the world. He'll give you the wisdom that people need to hear concerning their circumstances. For the most part, people in the world don't know what to do. Trust God and He'll use you to speak life into their situation and see things turn around. You'll be like Joseph who in a famine had the wisdom to store up grain for seven years. You'll be like Daniel whom the people said, "There's a man who knows what to do."

The Holy Spirit was not given so you'll have holy goosebumps and have a lot of fun. He's there to give you wisdom about things you know nothing about. You will impact the world around you in a good way when you are full of the Holy Spirit and wisdom, when inside of you is the spirit of excellence. God wants you to embrace the times and seasons. Don't just curse the darkness and walk away. No, bring the light of God with you and change the world you're in. God looked across time and intentionally put every man into the seasons they're living in. He then gave them the power and wisdom to do what needs to be done. People of excellence always sees the opportunity to make a positive impact in the middle of disorder. If you don't see things the right way, you won't respond the right way.

Even as bad as the world is sometimes, if you'll see bad situations as an opportunity to do good, you'll be able to say, "I was born for such a time as this" (Esther 4:14). Jesus said in John 12:27, "Now My soul is troubled, and what shall I say? 'Father, save Me from this hour'? No, it was for this reason I came to this hour." What was Jesus saying? "I was born for this! I was made for this moment." He encouraged Himself. He saw the cross but looked at the joy that followed. Heb. 12:2 says, "Who for the joy that was set before Him, endured the cross, despising the shame, and has sat down at the right hand of the throne of God." You'll be able to embrace your role in today's world when you realize that you were assigned by God to be in the place and season you're currently in.

Yes, life may get hard and persecution may come. What does Jesus say about this? "Stand up and lift up your heads because your redemption is drawing near" (Luke 21:28). This is called "living above the clouds." You're soaring like an eagle on the wind currents of the Holy Spirit. God is on your side and nothing can stop you now (Rom. 8:31). We're promised in Matt. 24:14, "And this gospel of the kingdom will be preached in the whole world as a testimony to all nations, and then the end will come." People of excellence stand up and say, "For I know that my Redeemer lives and that in the end He will stand on the earth" (Job 19:25). At the end of the age, when all is said and done, we win! You have to know this if you want to live a successful life by fulfilling your God-given destiny.

| 9 |

"BOND OF UNITY"

After praising God for telling him the king's dream along with its interpretation, Daniel is ushered into the king's presence where he again gives glory to God for revealing the dream. He said, "No wise man, enchanter, magician, or soothsayer can explain to the king the mystery he has asked about, but there is a God in heaven who reveals mysteries. He has made known to King Nebuchadnezzar what will be in the latter days" (Dan. 2:27,28). He then goes on to tell the dream in great detail. He describes a massive statue made of different materials which descended in value from the top to the bottom. Gold was at the top followed by silver, bronze, and iron mixed with clay at the bottom. This spectacular image was destroyed by a stone cut out without hands. What remained was blown away while the stone became a great mountain and filled the whole earth.

Nebuchadnezzar's kingdom was the head of gold and after him would come three other kingdoms each represented by the different materials he saw in his dream. These materials represent the Babylonian Empire, followed by the Medes and Persian Empire, the Greek Empire, and the Roman Empire. The stone represents the kingdom set up by God. This stone cut without hands is the Messiah, the Lord Jesus Christ. Ps. 118:22 says, "The stone which the builders rejected has become the chief cornerstone." Nebuchadnezzar then "fell on his face, prostrate before Daniel, and commanded that they should present an offering and incense to him" (vs. 46). The king answered Daniel and said, "Truly your God is the God of gods, the Lord of kings, and a revealer of mysteries, since you were able to reveal this mystery" (vs. 47).

What happens next is another miracle in the life of this spiritual giant when you consider he is a slave in a foreign land and was about to be executed the day before. Vs. 48, "Then the king promoted Daniel and gave him many great gifts; and he made him ruler over the whole province of Babylon." Not only that, he also became the "chief administrator over all the wise men of Babylon." Daniel was a humble man and he made sure his friends were also promoted. "Also Daniel petitioned the king, and he set Shadrach, Meshach, and Abed-Nego over the affairs of the province of Babylon; but Daniel sat in the court of the king" (vs.49). It was fitting that Daniel's friends got to share in his advancement because they accomplished much of the victory through their prayers. Men of excellence always appreciate their partners.

Scripture makes it quite clear that Daniel is deeply committed to these three friends of his. They came into captivity together and here they get promoted together. In Daniel's moment of exaltation, he didn't forget his friends who prayed with him when God revealed the details of the king's dream and its interpretation. Those with a spirit of excellence don't travel life alone but are open to God-ordained partnerships which are of paramount importance in one's work in the kingdom of God. A person's top priority is their relationship with God and, when they walk in excellence, they'll draw their close friends into this ongoing relationship with God. In Dan. 1:8 Daniel purposed in his heart not to defile himself by eating the king's delicacies and vs. 12 makes it clear his friends joined him in standing up for what was right.

This story of Daniel's friends joining him in not partaking of the king's food and wine reveals to us how much Daniel cared about the spiritual well-being of his friends. Daniel's chief concern was not about the social or dietary well-being of his friends. What concerned him most was the spiritual condition of their relationship with God. The bottom line is all children of God need one another. A Kenyan proverb says, "If you want to travel fast, travel alone. But if you want to travel far, travel together." People who travel alone and fast tend to burn out after a short while. To travel far, on the other hand, demands relationships with those who are on the same journey they're on. Daniel wanted to go far and he wanted his friends to go with him. He needed their prayers, support, and encouragement as he went forward.

Daniel loved his friends and wanted them to go far also. He wanted them to be just as successful as he wanted to be. He wanted to be there for them as they were for him. The role of a person of excellence is to help make the lives of other people better. This Daniel did when he asked the king to promote his friends also. Daniel made this request with graciousness of heart the same way he asked the chief of the eunuchs to let them eat vegetables instead of the king's food. An important test of character is how you accept praise and exaltation. Prov. 27:21 says, "Fire tests the purity of silver and gold, but a person is tested by being praised." Daniel had received great praise from King Nebuchadnezzar but he remained humble and submissive. For this reason, the king granted his request and his friends were promoted.

Daniel appeared to be the natural leader of these four men. It was he who took the initiative to go and negotiate with the chief of the eunuchs and later with the king. When the king granted him the time he requested, Daniel went to his friends and told them they were all going to to seek God for the interpretation of the dream. Building team dynamics is very important in our walk with the Lord. You can't get so far ahead of the people you're leading that they lose sight of you. If you pass over the horizon and there's no one behind you, it will appear you're on this journey alone. That's why good leadership requires maintenance of contact. Quite often you've got to look in the rear-view mirror so to speak and make sure your followers are still behind you. If not then you have to go back and get them.

When the children of Israel came out of Egypt they were led by a cloud by day and a pillar of fire by night. Both of these were always visible to the people. A good leader always stays in sight of the people. The children of Israel didn't have to send out a search party to find out where their leader was. Daniel was a good leader because he kept close to those under him. When he took the initiative, he made sure his friends were right there beside him. The goal of every good leader is to "present every man perfect in Christ Jesus" (Col. 1:28). Daniel cared about his friends and wanted to bring them to spiritual maturity. Being a good leader is a great privilege but it's also a great responsibility as well. A good shepherd always cares about the flock they're leading.

Be like Daniel and stir up your passion for others. Have a deep desire to take others with you as you travel down the path that leads to eternal life. Are your neighbors serving the Lord? Are your co-workers going to heaven? Care enough to find out and then act accordingly. Let your passion tell you what to do. It's this same passion, this spirit of togetherness, that drove Daniel to ask the king to promote his three friends also. Thankfully, the king granted his request. What happened next? We learn in Daniel 3 that the enemy has strategies to separate even when God brings people together in a bond of unity. Dan. 3:1 tells us King Nebuchadnezzar made a statue 90 feet tall and 9 feet wide. This image was much like the one he saw in his dream except this one was made completely of gold.

Many commentators feel that Nebuchadnezzar was trying to deify himself by making this statue in order to change the course of history and prolong the glory of his kingdom. He was still a pagan even though he had acknowledged the God of Daniel and his three friends was a God of wisdom and revelation. He shows no concern for the kings that will come after him. This is why there is no silver in the statue, nor bronze, iron, and clay. Nebuchadnezzar is only thinking of himself. He was told the dream and its interpretation was trustworthy, yet he still believed he could change the course of history. He arrogantly constructed this statue entirely of gold, in effect proclaiming himself as destined to be the greatest man in world history.

Ex. 20:3 says, "You shall have no other gods before Me." God says about idol worshipers, "These people are a stench in My nostrils, an acrid smell that never goes away" (Is. 65:5). Idols are a snare and a trap to those who worship and serve them. They lure people into practices that are repulsive, atrocious, and abominable to God. Ps. 106:36 says, "They served their idols, which became a snare to them." Ps. 115:8 says, "Those who make them are like them, so is everyone who trusts in them." It is interesting to note that the Bible says this statue was 60 cubits tall and 6 cubits wide. In the Bible the number 6 is the number of man who was created on the 6th day. The enemies of God are all marked by the number 6. Goliath was 6 cubits tall, had 6 pieces of armor, and a spear head weighing 6 hundred shekels of iron.

Solomon received in one year 666 talents of gold (1 Kings 10:14) and sat on a throne with only 6 steps (1 Kings 10:19). And we all know the mark of the beast is 666 (Rev. 13:18). Nebuchadnezzar set this statue up on the plain of Dura (vs. 1). The land was flat here so the statue would be visible from quite a distance. In 1863 the French archeologist Jules Oppert discovered a pedestal 6 miles SE of Babylon with dimensions 45' square and 20' in height. It is amazing that Nebuchadnezzar had just heard the word of God and he responds by building this statue. This shows he did not grasp the sovereignty of God over history. He then sent word to all of Babylon's dignitaries and had them gather at the dedication of this statue (vs. 2). He did this as a means to test their allegiance to him.

When all the officials had gathered at the statue a herald loudly proclaimed that when the music played all must fall down and worship the image of gold (Dan. 3:5). He then said, "And whoever does not fall down and worship shall be cast immediately into the midst of a burning fiery furnace" (vs. 6). The command to bow down before the image was followed by a powerful threat. Nebuchadnezzar regarded the refusal to worship the image as treasure for which you must die. To fall down is an act of submission. To worship means to bow down, to prostrate oneself in recognition and adulation before another. Idolatry is image worship. The call to worship indicates this is not a command to only show reverence and political allegiance but clearly has spiritual implications.

This command is going to affect every person of every language. Everyone is going to be put on the spot. Will they bow down and worship the image or will they not? All the Jews exiled in Babylon had faced indoctrination before but not persecution for their religious beliefs. To not obey will cost them their lives. The people of the land know Nebuchadnezzar was a ruthless man, showing no pity or compassion for others. He was not a man who allowed lawbreakers to go unpunished. Vs.

7 says that when all the people heard the sound of music, they all fell down and worshiped the golden image that Nebuchadnezzar the king had set up. In Hebrew this literally reads, "As soon as they were hearing they were falling down." This was total and immediate obedience to the king's command.

The people who bowed down to this statue were part of a godless culture, a culture that is driven by the flesh, a culture that wants nothing to do with God. This is clearly idolatry. These people feared King Nebuchadnezzar more than they feared God. Ps. 36:1 says, "There is no fear of God before their eyes." The universal corruption of every man ever born is the lack of fearing God, the wholesome dread of displeasing the almighty Creator of the universe. Charles Spurgeon says the evil men do is "the outer index of an inner evil. Unholiness is clear evidence of ungodliness. Despite the professions of unrighteous men, when we see their unhallowed actions our heart is driven to the conclusion that they have no religion whatever."

With wisdom he goes on to say, "If God is everywhere, and I fear Him, how can I dare to break His laws in His very presence?" Scripture repeatedly says we are to "fear the Lord and turn away from evil" (Prov. 3:7). It is "by the fear of the Lord one keeps away from evil" (Prov. 16:6). Why fear the Lord? Eccl. 12:14 says, "For God will bring every act to judgment, everything which is hidden, whether it is good or evil." Job set the standard for godly fear. Job 1:1 says, "There was a man in the land of Uz whose name was Job, and that man was blameless, upright, fearing God, and turning away from evil." When men no longer fear God, there is no holding back the fulfill-ment of their lusts. Rom. 3:18 (NLT) says, "They have no fear of God to restrain them."

The fear of the Lord is to depart from evil as you honor and obey God. John Calvin said, "In short, the fear of God is a bri-dle to restrain our wickedness." Theologian Robert Haldone said, "It is astonishing that men, while they acknowledge there is a God, should ac without any fear of His displeasure." The more you know God and respect Him, the more conscious you are of the dangers of ignoring who He is. Little knowledge leads to no respect and that is the road to disaster. The people of Babylon acted as if there was no God to whom they were ac-countable. Their behavior ignored the fact He has the power to punish them for their iniquity. Jesus said in Matt. 10:28, "Fear Him who is able to destroy both soul and body in hell." No wonder Prov. 23:17 says, "Live in the fear of the Lord always."

More than ever, a world that has turned its back on God need men and women with a spirit of excellence, believers who have the tenacity and faith to rise up out of the darkness. It needs people who are led by the Spirit of God, men and women who will stand up for what's right, men and women who will speak the voice of God wherever they may be. People of excellence know they're in the world but not of the world. They don't try to fit in with everybody else. They stand out in order to make a difference. Phil. 3:20 says, "Our citizenship is in heaven." This world is not our home, and all the followers of Christ have an assignment from Him to shine bright in a dark world. You are a citizen of an eternal kingdom. You live for something the world doesn't understand or comprehend. You live for something much bigger than what the world offers.

| 10 |

"A LIGHTED CANDLE"

The command had been given that when the music played all the people were to bow down and worship the golden image Nebuchadnezzar had set up. All across the plain of Dura a decision had to be made and the people only had two choices. They would either bow down before the image or burn in a fiery furnace. The music suddenly began to play and hundreds if not thousands of people fell on their faces and began to worship the towering image before them. These people feared the wrath of the king and their choice to bow down was made instantly. All the people obeyed the king's command. All, that is, except three. Daniel's three Hebrew friends, Shadrach, Meshach, and Abed-Nego were in the crowd and they must have asked themselves, "Is the fire in us greater than the furnace before us?"

Indeed it was and all three of them remained standing when everyone else bowed down. Their confidence in God caused them to not fear the wrath of the king. People of excellence know that what is burning inside of them is far greater and more powerful than anything the enemy can throw at them. All those with an excellent spirit must have the courage and the willingness to disobey the law of the land when it goes against what is being commanded by God. They're not afraid to go against the flow of what everyone else is doing. They want God's will to be done on earth as it is in heaven (Matt. 6:10). Men and women of excellence follow the example of Jesus. He was ridiculed, canceled, and criticized. Even death itself did not put out the fire that was on the inside of Him.

Shadrach, Meshach, and Abed-Nego did not bow because they refused to violate what their heart was telling them to do. Their conviction was greater than their compromise. Conviction is the product of one's relationship with God. The will to do what's right comes from the experiences they have with Him and through making Him the center of their lives. Your perception of God's nature, along with your vision of His purpose and your discernment of right and wrong, bring strength to your unwavering convictions. Your convictions reveal what you're made of on the day of trial. These three men were declaring by their bold stand of faith, "We don't bow! We don't bend! We don't compromise!" A person's eternal actions have their origin in God. In order to be a man or woman of excellence you must prepare yourself to stand strong by building strong convictions from within.

We must never waver in what we believe in. All over the world people are in a state of confusion and it takes people with godly convictions to lead them out of their confusion. Convictions come when you see God as an immediate and vitally important part of your life, when He becomes your "all in all" (1 Cor. 15:28). When you take a stand against compromise God will give you the Spirit-enabled desire and power to do what's right even when your life is threatened. Jesus said in Matt. 10:28, "Don't fear those who kill the body but are not able to kill the soul; rather fear Him who is able to destroy both soul and body in hell." MSG, "Don't be bluffed into silence by the threats of bullies. There's nothing they can do to your soul, your core being. Save your fear for God."

If you fear the furnace, if you fear the intimidation of those who want to hurt you, you will in time compromise the high standards you once walked in. People of excellence don't compromise. They're like Caleb who had a different spirit and followed God fully all the days of his life (Num. 14:24). Like Christ, Caleb came from the tribe of Judah. He had an unwavering trust in God. He was a warrior, a man of faith, a strong believer in the power of the God of Israel. He always stood his ground and was not discouraged by what others thought of him. He remained steadfast and refused to be influenced by the negative majority. He did not go along with the crowd who didn't believe God's promises. He was quick to exhibit faith as he boldly declared, "We are well able to take the land" (Num. 13:30).

Caleb refused to let the enemy live in the land God had given him. He did not let the giants who lived there cause him to compromise his convictions. Shadrach, Meshach, and Abed-Nego had the same type of spirit Caleb had. They had a conviction that even though the ultimatum was a fiery furnace, it made no difference. People are needed in the world today who will take a stand against compromise, people who will say, "If God be for us, who can be against us?" (Rom. 8:31). When captured by the Philistine army David said, "In God, whose word I praise, in God I have put my trust; I shall not be afraid. What can mere man do to me?" (Ps. 56:4). Know also that when you take a stand, the enemy will get very mad and try even harder to get you to compromise. In times like this you need confidence in chaos.

Wasting no time, some Babylonian officials went to the king and maliciously accused the three friends of Daniel of not bowing down to the golden image (Dan. 3:8). What was their motive for doing this? Jealousy. They were jealous because they were passed over when Shadrach, Meshach, and Abed-Nego were promoted over the affairs of Babylon. Jealousy is like a horrible cancer that eats nothing but its own heart. It was the sin of jealousy that caused Cain to rise up and murder his brother Abel. Jealousy consumes the soul of a man. Gen. 37:11 says it was jealousy that led Joseph's brothers to sell him as a slave to the Midianite traders. The most horrendous crime motivated by envy was the betrayal and crucifixion of Jesus. Matt. 27:18 says Pilate "knew that because of envy they had handed Him over."

Puritan Thomas Brooks said in the 17th century, "Envy tortures the affections, it vexes the mind, it inflames the blood, it corrupts the heart, it wastes the spirits." Driven by jealousy these officials said to Nebuchadnezzar, "O king, live forever!" (vs. 9). They then reminded him that those who did not bow would be met with a most severe penalty. They mentioned the three Hebrew men by name and told the king, "They do not serve your gods or worship the gold image which you have set up" (vs. 12). Shadrach, Meshach, and Abed-Nego must have known they would be discovered yet they obeyed God anyway. Charles Spurgeon said, "A lighted candle cannot be hid." Vs. 13, "Then Nebuchadnezzar, in rage and fury, gave the command to bring Shadrach, Meshach, and Abed-Nego. So they brought these men before the king."

As they were being taken to the king you can imagine God whispering in their ear, "Do not lose your confidence which has great reward" (Heb. 10:35). Don't throw away your confidence, hold onto it. Heb. 10:23 says, "Let us hold fast the confession of our hope without wavering, for He who promised is faithful." The Greek word for "confidence" is "parrhesia" and it conveys the idea of 'freedom to say all.' It is the attitude of openness that comes from freedom and lack of fear. Having confidence in chaos is courage manifested under persecution. It refers to boldness of speech. You'll say what's in your heart without fear and without reservation. Times of danger call for renewed confidence. It's what anchors the soul in hard times. To throw away confidence is to miss the reward confidence brings.

Shadrach, Meshach, and Abed-Nego were men of commitment and would not give in to external pressure. Their decision to remain standing was determined by inward principles. Ps. 57:7 says, "My heart is fixed, O God, my heart is fixed. I will sing and give praise." The NLT says, "My heart is confident in You,

O God, my heart is confident." Men and women who are committed are the people who change the world. They turn the world upside down (Acts 17:6) because people of commitment can't be stopped. Threats of death will not cause them to lose their confidence in the God they serve. They know God will stand with them if they dare to stand for Him. The threat of being thrown into a fiery furnace did not cause these three Jewish men to bow before the golden image because they had already bowed their hearts to God.

King Nebuchadnezzar clearly has an anger problem. He is full of rage and fury without knowing if the charges against these three men are true or not. Uncontrolled anger and resentment are like that. They're more often a mindless reaction rather than a responsible action after careful consideration. He asked the three men who now stood before him, "Is it true, Shadrach, Meshanch, and Abed-Nego, that you do not serve my gods or worship the golden image I have set up?" (vs. 14). David Guzik said, "It is one thing to make a stand for God; it is a greater thing to stick to your stand when pointedly asked, 'Is it true?'" Peter vowed to die for Christ yet he wilted and denied Jesus when asked, "Is it true?" If you cannot confess, "It is true," then do not profess to be His disciple.

Before the three men can answer if it is true or not, the king gives them a second chance to bow down before the image when the music plays. Here is one more temptation to compromise. The king clearly recognized the spiritual issues involved here. He knew that bowing down was to submit to the Babylonian gods. He then said, "But if you do not worship, you shall be cast immediately into the midst of a burning fiery furnace. And who is the god who will deliver you from my hands?" (vs. 15). His pride made him declare, "You shall have no other gods than me!" The god he really believed in was himself, not the gods of Babylon. Without a hint of a smile on his face he waited for their answer. Will they bow down to the golden image or not? Will they turn or burn?

Without hesitation the men said to the king, "O Nebuchadnezzar, we do not need to give you an answer concerning this matter." In other words, there is nothing to say. The ICB says, "Nebuchadnezzar, we do not need to defend ourselves to you." The MSG says, "Your threats mean nothing to us." It's true, "the righteous are bold as a lion" (Prov. 28:1). These three men may have read Isaiah's declaration written years before, "Behold, God is my salvation. I will trust and not be afraid, for the Lord God is my strength and song" (Is. 12:2). They also undoubtedly knew God's command in Ex. 20:3,5, "You shall have no other gods before Me. You shall not worship them or serve them; for I am a jealous God." These men would now bow to anyone or anything but the Almighty God of the universe. They know God never gives a command without also giving the enablement to obey it.

They were able to stand strong even when facing death by the all-sufficient grace of God which is magnified in times of persecution and difficulty (2 Cor. 12:10). For sure they remembered the delivering power of God when they made a choice with Daniel not to eat the king's food which would have defiled them (Dan. 1:8). They also remembered when they were delivered from being torn limb from limb (Dan. 2:12) when God revealed the mystery to Daniel when the four of them prayed. They stood strong because they feared God and trusted Him. The fear of the Lord is the best antidote for neutralizing the fear of man and the worst that man can do to you. In a trial fix your eyes on the promises of God. Is. 43:2 says, "When you walk through the fire, you will not be scorched, nor will the flames burn you."

They told the king, "If it be so, our God whom we serve is able to deliver us from the burning fiery furnace, and He will deliver us from your hand, O King" (vs. 17). They affirmed their faith and trust in God by saying, "He is able." It was this confidence that allowed them to look death in the eye and not flinch. They feared not the wrath of the king because by faith they had an eye on Him who is invisible (Heb. 11:27), the one who "will deliver us from your hand." Years earlier David told King Saul, "The Lord who delivered me from the paw of the lion and the paw of the bear, He will deliver me from the hand of this Philistine" (1 Sam. 17:37). Ps. 121:7,8, "The Lord will protect you from all evil; He will keep your soul. The Lord will guard your going out and your coming in from this time forth and forever."

God had prepared these Jewish lads for "such a time as this" (Esther 4:14) by having them remember His promises, His past deliverances, and His commands that include His enablements. This was a matter of life and death and no room was left to question what was the right thing to do. The thought of bowing down was not to be considered. They were ready to burn rather than betray their God. Charles Spurgeon said, "To hold fast a clear conscious is the rarest jewel which can adorn the bosom of a mortal." Their example "is well calculated to excite in the mind of believers firmness and steadfastness in upholding the truth in the teeth of tyranny and in the very jaws of death." When you see no way out of a bad situation, walk by faith and not by sight (2 Cor. 5:7). Do God the honor to trust Him when it comes to matters of loss for the sake of principle.

Shadrach, Meshach, and Abed-Nego had one message for King Nebuchadnezzar and one message only. Men of excellence do not bow! Period! Case closed! End of story! By faith these lads committed themselves to God and now God commits Himself to them. He gives them the boldness and strength to stand and defy the king. They then said, "But if not, let it be known to you, O King, that we do not serve your gods, nor will we worship the gold image which you have set up" (vs. 18). Many false teachings have gone out over these three words, "But if not..." They say these three men thought there was a chance God might not deliver them. This simply is not true. They said in vs. 17 that God would deliver them. To say He might not deliver them is doubt and surely they would have died that day.

What they were saying is, "If you throw us into the furnace God will deliver us. But if not, if you don't throw us into the furnace, we still won't worship your gods." They had yielded their hearts to God and this paved the way for a miracle to take place. It is inconceivable to say they believed in anything different than total deliverance. Of course, this didn't go over very well with the king. Vs. 19 says, "Nebuchadnezzar was full of fury and his face changed toward Shadrach, Meshach, and Abed-Nego." When you don't compromise with people, their attitude toward you will change. It's when you stand up for what's right that you'll find out who your friends really are. Nebuchadnezzar commanded the furnace to be made seven times hotter than usual. He then commanded the three men to be bound and cast into the fiery furnace (vs. 21).

| 11 |

"SWEET MELODY"

King Nebuchadnezzar is clearly out of his mind. He commanded Shadrach, Meshach, and Abed-Nego to be thrown into a fiery burning furnace because they would not bow. Imagine the king's face. Bright red! Nostrils flaring! Anger is an ugly thing not to mention that a distorted face usually resorts in distorted judgment. To increase their pain, he ordered the furnace to be heated seven times hotter than unusual. This makes no sense for this is the opposite of what he should have done. If he wanted to make the deaths of these young men more painful, he should have turned the furnace down because it would have prolonged their agony. The enemy's kingdom is a kingdom of darkness and what he did has no reason to it. Eccl. 7:9 says, "Do not be eager in your heart to be angry, for anger resides in the bosom of fools."

The king has no light in him. He has no clarity so he's chaotic. He commanded his strongest warriors to bind the lads as if they were actually going to be able to escape. So irrational was the king's decision to heat the furnace up that when these warriors opened the doors to throw in the men of God they themselves died because of the intense heat (Dan. 3:22). The good news is the fire inside Shadrach, Meshach, and Abed-Nego was hotter than all the furnaces in the world. It was a fire that would never be put out. This was a spiritual battle for sure, and these young men would not be intimidated. Despite the intense intimidation, they stayed courageous in their confession of faith. Poet Annie Johnson Flint wrote, "He gives more grace when the burdens grow greater. He sends more strength when the labors increase." That's the God we serve.

In a culture of chaos, the world needs people of excellence who are bold as a lion, men and women who have so much confidence that they'll sleep peacefully in a storm. Their confidence won't waver if they face a giant like David, if they end up in a pit like Joseph, or are thrown into a fiery furnace like Shadrach, Meshach, and Abed-Nego. They have confidence because they know God is always with them. No matter what they go through, God always prepares a table for them in the presence of their enemies (Ps. 23:5). A puritan once wrote, "Of all graces, faith renders the soul most invincible and therefore you should labor above all to be rich in faith. It renders the soul invincible and unconquerable under all the hardships and trials which it meets with in this world."

Faith makes a person of excellence triumph in all the trials and challenges of life. It was the faith of Shadrach, Meshach, and Abed-Nego that made them invincible as the king was about to find out. Dan. 3:23 says they "fell into the midst of the furnace of blazing fire still tied up." Then something strange happened.

Vs. 24 says, "Then King Nebuchadnezzar was astonished." In Hebrew the word "astonished" means 'startled, alarmed, to be bewildered with an element of fear because of an amazing or fearful sight or a terrifying sound.' What caused the king to be so startled? The Greek translation of the Hebrew New Testament reads the king "heard them singing praises" unto the Lord their God. These men are singing a supernatural song and the king can't believe his ears. One is reminded of Paul and Silas singing praises in the midst of the Philippian jail (Acts 16:25).

The devil loves to get men to compromise. What he doesn't tell you is that anything you compromise godly principles to get, you'll ultimately lose. Compromise is probably the number one sin the people of God are involved in. Paul said in 1 Cor. 15:34 that if you'll awake to righteousness, you'll sin not. Why compromise if you know God is on your side? Why compromise if you know "that all things work together for the good to those who love God" (Rom. 8:28)? Shadrach, Meshach, and Abed-Nego knew that they knew God would deliver them from the fiery burning furnace, that if they didn't bow, they wouldn't burn. Ps. 34:19 says, "Many are the afflictions of the righteous, but the Lord delivers him out of them all." That's a promise to stand on when the furnace is turned up seven times hotter.

Ps. 34:20 (MSG), "He's your bodyguard, shielding every bone; not even a finger gets broken." For this reason, you don't compromise when the heat is on. Why bow if no weapon formed against you will prosper (Is. 54:17)? Why bow if you know nothing can separate you from the love of Christ (Rom. 8:35)? Why bow if greater is He who is in you is greater than he who is in the world (1 John 4:4)? Why bow if whatever is born of God overcomes the world (1 John 5:4)? Why bow if you can do all things through Christ who strengthens you (Phil. 4:13)? Why bow knowing nothing will be impossible with God (Luke 1:37)? Did Shadrach, Meshach, and Abed-Nego bow? No! Did they doubt? No! Did they fear? No! Instead, they sang a sweet melody that reached the ears of God.

It can be rightfully assumed that when Nebuchadnezzar had the three Hebrew lads thrown into the fire he believed they would be immediately consumed. With a look of satisfaction on his face he was ready to put the matter behind him but was stopped by the sound of singing coming from the furnace. In his astonishment Nebuchadnezzar stood up in haste and said to his high officials, "Was it not three men we cast bound into the midst of the fire?" (Dan. 3:24). They said, "Certainly, O king" to which he replied, "Look! I see four men loosed and walking about in the midst of the fire without harm" (vs. 25). The king is startled because there are now four men in the fire instead of three, not one of them are bound, they're walking around in the fire, and all of them are unhurt.

Charles Spurgeon said, "Shadrach, Meshach, and Abed-Nego lost something in the fire. The fire did not hurt them, but it snapped their bonds. Blessed loss! A true Christian's losses are gains in another shape. Many of God's servants never know the fullness of spiritual liberty till they are cast into the midst of the furnace." Now comes the shocker as King Nebuchadnezzar tells us who the fourth person in the fire is, "And the form of the fourth is like the Son of God" (vs. 25). The fourth person in the furnace was Jesus Christ in one of His many pre-incarnate appearances in the Old Testament, those select times when He manifested Himself on the earth. For sure Nebuchadnezzar did not expect to see the same person who appeared in the Garden of Eden, walked with Enoch, feasted with Abraham, and wrestled with Jacob.

Who is this fourth man? In Genesis He's the Seed of woman. In Exodus He's the Passover Lamb and in Leviticus He's our High Priest. In Numbers He's our Pillar of Cloud by day and Pillar of Fire by night. In Deuteronomy He is the Prophet like unto Moses and in Joshua He's the Captain of our salvation. In Judges He's our Judge and Lawgiver and in Ruth He's our Kinsman. In 1 and 2 Samuel He's our Trusted Prophet and in 1 and 2 Kings He's our Reigning King. In Ezra He's our Faithful Scribe and in Nehemiah He's the Builder of broken down walls and human lives. In Esther He's our Mordecai and in Job He's our Forever Living Redeemer. In Psalms He's our Shepherd and in Proverbs He's our Wisdom. In the Song of Solomon He's our Lover and Bridegroom and in Isaiah He's the Prince of Peace.

In Jeremiah He's the Righteous Branch and in Lamentations He's the Weeping Prophet. In Ezekiel He's the wonderful Four-Faced Man and in Hosea He's the Faithful Husband. In Amos He's our Burden Bearer and in Obadiah He's the One who is mighty to save. In Jonah He's our Foreign Missionary and in John He's the Baptizer bringing us to the Father. In Micah He's the Messenger with beautiful feet and in Nahum He's the

Avenger on His enemies. In Habakkuk He is God's Evangelist and in Zephaniah He's our Savior. In Haggai He's the Re-
storer of God's lost heritage. In Zechariah He's the Fountain
that opens the house of David and in Malachi He's the Son of
Righteousness. In Matthew He's the Messiah and in Mark He's
the Wonder Worker. In Luke He's the Son of Man and in John
He's the Son of God. In Acts He's the Disciple reaching the
whole world.

Who is this fourth man? In Romans He's the Justifier. In 1
and 2 Corinthians He's the Santifier. In Galatians He's the Redeemer from the curse of the law. In Ephesians He's the Christ
with unsearchable riches. In Philippians He's the God who
supplies all your needs. In Colossians He's the fullness of the
Godhead bodily. In 1 and 2 Thessalonians He's our soon coming King. In 1 and 2 Timothy He's the Mediator between God
and man. In Titus He's our Faithful Pastor. In Philemon He's
the Friend who sticks closer than a brother. In Hebrews He's
the Blood of an everlasting covenant. In James He's our Great
Physician. In 1 and 2 Peter He's the Chief Shepherd. In 1,2,3
John He is love. In Jude He's the Lord coming with ten thousands of His saints.

Who is the fourth man? In Revelation He's the King of kings
and Lord of lords. He's the one who stands in the fiery furnace
with you when you refuse to compromise. Who is He? He's
Abel's sacrifice, Noah's rainbow, and Abraham's ram. He's
Isaac's well, Jacob's scepter, Moses' rod, and Joshua's sun and
moon. He's Elijah's mantle, Elisha's staff, and Gideon's fleece.
He's Samuel's horn of oil, David's slingshot, Hezekiah's sun-

dial, and Daniel's vision. Who is this fourth man? He's Peter's shadow, Stephen's signs and wonders, and Paul's handkerchief. He's John's pearly white city. He's the Father to the orphan and Husband to the widow. He is the Traveler in the night, the Bright and Morning Star. He's the Lily of the Valley, the Rose of Sharon, the Honey in the rock, the Image of God's glory.

After spending time with Jesus, Daniel's three friends were summoned out of the fiery furnace by a stunned King Nebuchadnezzar who came and stood at the door. He said, "Shadrach, Meshach, and Abed-Nego, come out, you servants of the Most High God, and come here!" (Dan. 3:26). The three men obeyed and came out of the fire. Notice that Nebuchadnezzar recognizes that these three lads, these three men of excellence, serve the Most High God even before they are out of the furnace. These men walked by faith and not by sight (2 Cor. 5:7). They became living epistles (2 Cor. 3:2) that pointed to a supernatural God who even Nebuchadnezzar was forced to acknowledge. When we stand for Christ, He stands with us. The world receives a witness through our stand regardless if they surrender to Him or not.

All people of excellence should be encouraged by this. By their one act of steadfast faith they became a witness for the living God to the entire Babylonian Empire. In other words, God will always use the furnace of adversity for His purpose. Joseph told his brothers, "What you meant for evil, God meant for good" (Gen. 50:20). Let your confidence grow knowing that every pit, every prison, every persecution, every Goliath, and every furnace will be used for the glory of God. All the king's officials gathered around and saw that the fire had no effect on these men. Their hair was not singed, their clothes were not damaged, and the smell of smoke was not upon them. This was a total and complete deliverance. They were not merely delivered from the fire, they were delivered through the fire because Jesus was there with them.

Charles Spurgeon said, "Though the smell of fire had not passed on them, I feel sure that it left a glow on their countenances and a glory on their persons." All men and women of excellence should have a glow on their face for all the world to see. This glow will make them like a city on a hill that can't be hidden (Matt. 5:14). Nebuchadnezzar responded and said, "Blessed be the God of Shadrach, Meshach, and Abed-Nego, who sent His Angel and delivered His servants who put their trust in Him" (vs. 28). Nebuchadnezzar, the idol worshipping king, had acknowledged God in Dan. 2:47 as the "revealer of mysteries" and in Dan. 3:29 as the God "who is able to deliver." He gave glory to God, the Most High God, but he did not say this God was His God. He knew a lot about God but did not yet know Him personally.

He did, however, give recognition that He is the God of these three brave men, that He is a God of great power, a God worthy of trust, a God worthy of full surrender and exclusive allegiance. He said, "They have frustrated the king's word, and yielded their bodies, that they should not serve nor worship any god except their own God" (vs. 28). They surrendered themselves completely to God - spirit, soul, and body. Rom. 12:1 says, "Present your bodies a living sacrifice, holy, acceptable to God, which is your reasonable service." Men and women of excellence resist the temptation to bow and forever pursue God's ideal. They are not conformed to this world but are transformed by the renewing of their mind (Rom. 12:2). People in the world are greatly impacted when they see men and women of excellence in fiery trials yet do not panic. That is when they see Jesus living in them and through them.

Impacted by all this, Nebuchadnezzar made a decree through the land that everybody must speak well of their God or they will be cut in pieces (Dan. 3:29). And then in vs. 30 he promotes them to a higher position and authority in the land. The very thing he used to demote them becomes the very place where he promotes them. There is no man-made furnace that can change your God-given purpose. You need to possess your inheritance and stop doubting what God says is yours to possess. Inside of you is the spirit of excellence that gives you the confidence to stand when facing a burning furnace when everyone else bows down or runs away. You need not fear the furnace because the fire in you is far greater than the fire before you. You'll come out of it better than when you went into it.

You won't even smell of smoke. Your passion will be stronger for there will be an awakening again of your heavenly calling and your destiny to fulfill. All the days of your life you'll come against the intimidation of the enemy. In the midst of chaos you'll have clarity knowing what God wants you to do. God has given you a land to possess and to do that you must have the boldness of a lion. You must be like Shadrach, Meshach, and Abed-Nego. Their story should encourage you to stand up for righteousness regardless of the consequences for we do not know the impact our stand might have on others. They changed the world they lived in and you can do the same. All you have to do is say what Joshua said. "As for me and my house, we will serve the Lord" (Josh. 24:15).

| 12 |

"THE MERCY OF GOD"

The world we live in is changing at a rapid pace and all men and women of excellence need to know how to navigate their lives in the midst of a very pagan, shifting culture. Gross sin that was shunned a short time ago has now become the norm. Good is bad and bad is good. Men want to be women and women want to be men. What should we do in the midst of all this? How should we act? What stand should we take? Thankfully, the Bible answers those questions for us in the book of Daniel. One of the greatest playbooks for the answers to these questions is found during the time of Daniel where a negative cultural change already happened. The nation of Israel was taken into a pagan, ungodly culture called Babylon. They became slaves because of their constant rejection of God and His principles.

We are given throughout the book of Daniel principle after principle of how we're to live in the same type of ungodly culture from a generation that already had to do it. The entire book of Daniel is set in Babylon. The spirit of Babylon was on the earth long before the city was ever built, and it's still on the earth today. In the Garden of Eden the devil showed up and asked Eve, "Did God really say?" (Gen. 3;1). The first words out of the devil's mouth was to question God. He later deceived Eve into doing what she wanted instead of what God wanted and this is the spirit of Babylon. He wants you to think that life is all about me, myself, and I. The same thing happened at Babel where the people said, "Come, let us build ourselves a city, with a tower that reaches to the heavens, so that we can make a name for ourselves" (Gen. 11:4).

Gen. 11:11, "Therefore its name is called Babel because there the Lord confused the language of the whole world." The word "Babel" is where the word "Babylon" comes from. The word "Babel" literally means 'sown in confusion.' When you buy into the lie that the world revolves around you and what you want, there will be confusion. If there is one thing that could classify the culture we live in today, it's that people are very confused while at the same time being very disturbed. People today are more mentally depressed, full of anxiousness, anxiety, fear, and intimidation than ever before because they bought into the Babylonian lie. The sin of pride is the greatest sin ever. It's the sin that got Lucifer kicked out of heaven (Is. 14:14) and it will keep millions of people out of heaven as well.

Consider Is. 47:8, "Now then, listen, you lover of pleasure, lounging in your security and saying to yourself, 'I am, and there is no one else besides me.'" Vs. 10, "You have trusted in your wickedness and have said, 'No one sees me.' Your wisdom and knowledge warped you and led you astray." To summarize it all in one sentence, the Babylon mentality elevates self and lowers God. It tells you to do whatever you want and forget what God wants. The spirit of Babylon is pride and the world today celebrates that. All the time people say, "I'm going to do what I want and don't care what you think." Being full of pride didn't turn out too well for the devil and we are going to see in Daniel 4 that neither did the pride mentality turn out well for Nebuchadnezzar.

After witnessing the miraculous deliverance of the three Hebrew lads from the fiery furnace, Nebuchadnezzar makes a proclamation about how great God is. He said in Dan. 4:3, "How great are His signs, and how mighty His wonders! His kingdom is an everlasting kingdom, and His dominion is from generation to generation." Nebuchadnezzar was a great king but here he recognized that God's kingdom was far greater and His dominion was completely unique because it is an everlasting kingdom. He was greatly impressed with the all powerful majesty of God. For sure, He is the King of all nations, His dominion is everlasting, and every generation is proof of His influence. This is his royal proclamation, his personal witness of the saving power of the Most High God. He is not ashamed to share this testimony with the entire known world.

This is all well and good, and surely God should be praised. However, Nebuchadnezzar is a man filled with pride and trouble will soon be forthcoming. He said in Dan. 4:4, "I, Nebuchadnezzar, was at rest in my house and flourishing in my palace." This ease he was having is the false security of the ungodly. This false peace was deceptive as it is with all the rich and powerful who are not in right standing with God. Prosperity is a dangerous thing for it often produces pride. Prov. 16:18 says, "Pride goes before destruction, and a haughty spirit before a fall." Let us never forget what prosperity and pride did to Saul and Solomon. This was a deceitful rest which has the power to give you a false sense of security. To be at peace does not prove all is well. To be untroubled is no evidence of safety.

Nebuchadnezzar was basking in self-satisfaction. He was very content and prosperous and one night he went to bed expecting to have dreams about wealth, luxury, and splendor. Little did he know that God had other plans. Instead of a happy dream he had a dream that "made me afraid, and the thoughts on my bed and the visions of my head troubled me" (vs. 5). Nebuchadnezzar was a mighty king and was not in the habit of being afraid. Yet this dream was given to him for that very purpose. God saw that he needed to be troubled. A troubled soul is always attached to everything that has to do with pride. Nebuchadnezzar was about to take a hard fall and God was warning him this would happen. Like he did with the first dream he called in his enchanters and magicians but this time he told them the dream instead of making them tell him what the dream was.

Vs. 7 says these counselors did not make known the interpretation to the king. The dream was fairly easy to interpret but these wise men lacked courage more than insight. Nebuchadnezzar said they would not make known the interpretation, not that they could not make it known. So what does he do? He calls in Daniel. Ungodly men always call on God as a last resort when everything else fails. He then did a despicable thing by saying, "His name is Beltashazzar, according to the name of my god" (vs. 8). Despite his prior revelations of the one true God, he still considered the Babylonian deity Bel to be his god. He was impressed with God but not enough to be converted. Still, he clearly recognized there was something different about Daniel. He said, "In him is the Spirit of the Holy God, and I related the dream to him" (vs. 8).

Nebuchadnezzar begins by saying in the dream there was a lush and magnificent "tree in the midst of the earth and its height was great. The tree grew and became strong; It's height reached the heavens, and it could be seen to the ends of all the earth. Its leaves were lovely and its fruit abundant, and in it was food for all. The beasts of the field found shade under it and the birds of the sky dwelt in its branches" (vs. 10-12). So far everything in this dream is well and good. The tree in Nebuchadnezzar's dream was noted for its size, strength, prominence, fruit, and shelter. Suddenly something strange happened. Vs. 13 says, "I was looking in the visions in my mind as I lay on my bed, and behold, an angelic watcher, a holy one, descended from heaven."

This "watcher" was an angel from heaven and the term "holy one" describes 'one set apart for a special purpose.' In this case his purpose was to deliver a message to the king. Angels are forever on the watch to execute God's will. Ps. 103:20 says, "Bless the Lord, you His angels, mighty in strength, who perform His word, obeying the voice of His word." The angels of heaven possess great wisdom (2 Sam. 14:20), great strength (Ps.

103:20), great speed (Dan. 9:21), and are great in number (Heb. 12:22). They were created to be ministering spirits continually sent forth to serve and minister to those who shall be heirs of salvation (Heb. 1:14). They accomplish their ministry in various ways, including bringing instruction (Acts 10:3-6), deliverance (Ps. 34:7), comfort (Matt. 1:20), and reception at death (Luke 16:22).

This mighty angel cried aloud abruptly and without warning and explained that the great tree which was seemingly indestructible is to be chopped down. He said, "Chop down the tree and cut off its branches, strip off its leaves, and scatter its fruit. Let the beasts flee from under it, and the birds from its branches" (vs. 14). The destruction would have been complete except for what the angel said next, "Yet leave the stump with its roots in the ground, bound with a band of iron and bronze" (vs. 15). Leaving the stump with its roots implies that even though the tree is chopped down it is not completely destroyed. This speaks of the potential for revival. This is the mercy of God. He'll cut you down because of pride but He'll give you a chance to come right back up if you'll repent and make right decisions again.

The tree's life-giving root is spared and bound with a band of iron and bronze. This will keep the stump firm, protecting it from splitting and natural deterioration. The angel continues, "And let him be drenched with the dew of heaven, and let him graze with the beasts on the grass of the earth. Let his mind be changed from that of a man, let him be given the mind of a beast, and let seven years pass over him" (vs. 15,16). Following the ways of the devil never puts you in a good place. Instead, you'll be cut down and crawl on your belly as you eat grass like a wild animal. The good news is that God is always a merciful, loving, and forgiving God. He'll pick you up and cause you to prosper again if you'll only acknowledge that the Most High rules (vs. 17).

This was a very disturbing dream and the difficulty was not in its interpretation, it's in telling the king that this prophetic dream is about him. Surely the magicians feared for their lives. If they told the king he was about to go insane and become like a wild animal, almost for certain they'd be put to death. But Daniel had no such fear. He still, however, had to prioritize the way he presented the interpretation to the king. This was a big assignment and he had to do it right. Men of excellence always speak the truth in love (Eph. 4:15). To be effective, the person hearing the truth must know they're being loved by the person telling them the truth. It's true, it's not what you say that matters, it's how you say it. Even if what you say is true, you can't go around pointing your finger at people while shouting, "Thus says the Lord!"

You must speak with a genuine care for the person you're talking to. When you speak for God you must do so with humility and graciousness for this is what allows God to use you. It is a tremendous privilege to speak the oracles of God (1 Peter 4:11), those supernatural utterances inspired by God that are extremely wise and received as authoritative. The judgment of God is about to come down on Nebuchadnezzar and Daniel had to tell him this all the while knowing what an angry and unpredictable man he was. Daniel knew it was better to fear God than man. He also knew God is a good God and he hoped in his heart that the words he speaks will pave the way for the recovery God wants to bring. Wherever you speak about the judgment of God, you must also speak about the mercy of God. He is a loving God who always forgives and brings transformation to those who asks Him to.

Daniel is troubled as he weighs the words of the king. What bothered Nebuchadnezzar is now bothering him, so much so that he is told by the king to not let the dream trouble him (vs. 19). Daniel wants to choose his words with care, not like those who use "their tongues as weapons, flinging poison words, poison-tipped arrow-words not caring who they hit" (Ps. 64:3,4). If spoken wrongly, words can be sharp and do great damage. Bitter words are like fire in the bones and can make any situation far worse than it already is. Men and women with an excellent spirit listen carefully and caringly. They weigh the words spoken to them with care all the while thinking of ways to respond appropriately. They know that "out of the abundance of the heart the mouth speaks" (Luke 6:45). The overflow of what has been stored in your heart will be heard in your words.

Don't be like the fool who thinks he can hide what's in his heart, who thinks he can say something on the outside that is different than how he feels on the inside. It's not going to happen. Somehow, some way, the person he's talking to will hear and receive what is in abundance in the man's heart no matter what he says. People have a way of knowing whether or not you're trying to cover up how you really feel by speaking smooth words that are dipped in honey. Great damage is done when people say things they shouldn't say. They also get hurt when people say things that need to be said without a caring, genuine love in their heart. Daniel, a man with an excellent spirit, hesitated briefly before interpreting the dream for the king because he wanted to make sure his heart was where it should be.

Responding with care, Daniel said in Dan. 4:19, "My lord, may the dream concern those who hate you, and its interpretation concern your enemies!" He wished the dream was not about the king even though he knew that it was. He then repeated the dream back to the king and said, "It is you O king, who have grown and become strong" (vs. 22). He tells how a holy one comes from heaven and says in vs. 25,26, "They shall drive you from men, your dwelling shall be with the beasts of the field and they shall make you eat grass like oxen. They shall wet you with the dew of heaven, and seven years shall pass over you, till you know that the Most High rules in the kingdom of men and gives it to whomever He chooses. And inasmuch as they gave the command to leave the stump and roots of the tree, your kingdom shall be assured to you, after you come to know that Heaven rules."

There is no easy way to break bad news to people. You just have to be honest and straight forward. If you're not honest and open with people, the more painful it becomes. Don't be insensitive when you give bad news to people. Care what they're going through. "Weep with those who weep" (Rom.

12:15). Look for ways to sow hope into the situation. Bring something positive when you speak to grieving people. Daniel told the king that after his seven year ordeal, his kingdom would be there waiting for him. Daniel also knew this was a good time to be evangelistic, to bring a good word in due season. He said, "Therefore, O king, let my counsel be acceptable to you. Break off your sins by being righteous, and your iniquities by showing mercy to the poor. Perhaps there may be a lengthening of your prosperity" (vs. 27).

| 13 |

"SECOND CHANCE"

G od revealed to Nebuchadnezzar in a dream that he was about to be severely judged because of his rebellious pride and his "there is no god besides me" arrogance. Merciful as God is, He had Daniel tell the king that the right reaction to the threat of judgment is humble repentance. The king either had to repent or be chopped down. At this time courageous confrontation was necessary. Daniel told him, "Break away from your sins by being righteous, and from your iniquities by showing mercy to the poor" (Dan. 4:27). The hammer of the Lord is about to come down and Nebuchadnezzar was not only counseled to stop sinning but also to practice righteousness and generosity. Daniel calls on the king to have a change of heart and repent. If he would do so, Daniel said, "Perhaps there may be a lengthening of your prosperity" (vs. 27).

Daniel is telling Nebuchadnezzar that he doesn't have to wait to go insane to make things right with God. He could repent now and escape the coming judgment upon him. God was going to wipe out Nineveh because of the abundance of wickedness there but first He sent Jonah to preach a message of repentance to them. Jonah 3:10 says, "Then God saw their works, that they turned from their evil way, and God relented from the disaster that He said He would bring upon them." Surely the same thing could happen to Nebuchadnezzar if he did what the people of Nineveh did, if he turned from his wicked ways and sought the Lord diligently. Daniel was saying, "Repent now from your pride and arrogance and your kingdom won't get cut down. You can do in seven minutes what will take seven years if you don't repent."

Unfortunately, Nebuchadnezzar didn't give heed to the warning the dream gave him and he went about business as usual. He should have repented then and there but he didn't. Time passes and twelve months later he's walking on the roof of the royal palace of Babylon where he sees the splendor of his kingdom spread out before him. Babylon was truly one of the spectacular cities of the ancient world which included the famous Hanging Gardens built during the reign of Nebuchadnezzar. There is a recorded prayer he once prayed to his god Marduk, "Like dear life I love thy exalted lodging place. In no place have I made a town more glorious than thy city of Babylon." God had given him a full year to repent and he probably forgot about the dream during that time. When judgment did not come at once, he returned to his arrogant ways.

Words of pride spill from his mouth, "Is not this the great Babylon I have built as the royal residence by my mighty power and for the glory of my majesty?" (vs. 30). His repeated self-affirmation emphasizes his self-centered state. Here is a classic illustration of a man boasting in what he thinks he can do apart from God. Even as the words are still on his lips, a voice came from heaven, saying, "King Nebuchadnezzar, to you it is spoken: your royal authority has been taken from you" (vs. 31). His dream is about to come to pass. "Immediately what had been said about Nebuchadnezzar was fulfilled. He was driven away from people and ate grass like an ox. His body was drenched with the dew of heaven until his hair grew like the feathers of an eagle and his nails like the claws of a bird" (vs. 33).

Nebuchadnezzar is not in a good place and neither is anybody else who walks away from God. Nothing the devil offers you will take you to a good place. There will be sadness in your soul and confusion all around you when you walk in darkness and not in the light. Like the rest of the world, you'll look for solutions in all the wrong places. Thankfully, there is a way to get your life back on track. Dan. 4:34,35, "At the end of that time, I, Nebuchadnezzar, raised my eyes toward heaven, and my sanity was restored. Then I praised the Most High; I honored and glorified Him who lives forever. His dominion is an eternal dominion; His kingdom endures from generation to generation. All the peoples of the earth are regarded as nothing. He does as He pleases with the powers of heaven and the peoples of the earth. No one can hold back His hand" (vs. 35).

Nebuchadnezzar acknowledged God and he said in vs. 36, "At the same time that my sanity was restored, my honor and splendor were returned to me for the glory of my kingdom." What people don't know about God is that if you'll repent and turn from your wicked ways, He'll always return you back to a better place than you were before. He'll restore your honor for the glory of your kingdom, the glory of your family, your job, your life. All He asks is you don't get prideful and give Him all the glory. After being humbled Nebuchadnezzar said, "My advisers and nobles sought me out and I was restored to my throne and became greater than before" (vs. 36). God gave him a second chance. If the Babylon mentality is inside you, if every part of your life is sown in confusion, do what Nebuchadnezzar did and God will also give you a second chance.

What did Nebuchadnezzar do next? He said, "Now I praise and exalt and glorify the King of heaven, because everything He does is right and all His ways are just" (vs. 37). He next said something he learned very well from his seven years of living like an animal, "And those who walk in pride He is able to humble" (vs. 37). Do you want your sanity back? Do you want your wayward mind restored and all the confusion taken out of your life? It will happen when you, first of all, exalt the King of heaven. Not only do men of excellence exalt God as God, they exalt Him as King! The kingdom of God is not a democracy, it's a kingdom and in a kingdom the king rules. We are ruled by the King of kings and our opinion doesn't count. We don't get a vote in things pertaining to the kingdom for it's only His will and purpose that matters.

When you understand that, you'll willingly submit to His rule and authority knowing that He'll raise you up and place you into His royal family forevermore. This is why David said in Ps. 145:1,2, "I will exalt You, my God the King; Every day I will bless You, and I will praise Your name forever and ever." Kingdoms don't have opinions, they have absolutes. Many people love God's attributes and don't like His absolutes not realizing God is not giving them a choice in the matter. So what do you do? You submit your life to God. You bow before Him and offer yourself to Him as "a living sacrifice, holy and acceptable to God" (Rom. 12:1). You honor Him and submit to Him because He's the King. If you want your sanity back, submit to the King. Say to Him, "Not my will but Your will be done in my life" (Luke 22:42).

You will also get your sanity back when you acknowledge that God does everything right and all His ways are just. That includes the part you don't like or understand. Some people may say, "I don't know if I agree with that." It doesn't matter if they agree or not. The truth is what God calls the truth and sin is what God calls sin. Is. 55:7 says, "Let the wicked forsake their ways and the unrighteous their thoughts. Let them turn to the Lord and He will have mercy on them." God said in Is. 55:9, "For as the heavens are higher than the earth, so are My ways above your ways, and My thoughts than your thoughts." Pastor Tim Keller once said, "If your god never disagrees with you, you might just be worshiping an idealized version of yourself."

Finally, walk in humility. You will get your sanity back when you decide to not make life all about you. Follow God and let Him be the Lord of your life. John the Baptist said it best, "I must decrease, He must increase" (John 3:30). All forms of selfishness must be abandoned so God can rule and reign in your life. Pride says, "I don't need God. I am God." Humility says, "I need God. I am nothing without Him." We read in Acts 17:28,

"In Him I live and move and have my being." Fear God and tremble before Him. He said in Is. 66:2, "This is the one I esteem: he who is humble and contrite in spirit, and trembles at My word." In life you're either going to have humility or humiliation as Nebuchadnezzar found out as he was eating grass like an ox. Don't let that happen to you. Be humble at all times.

When we come to Daniel 5 Nebuchadnezzar is no longer king. The ancient historian Berosus tells us that he died after a 43-year reign. Belshazzar is now king and was Nebuchadnezzar's grandson through his daughter Nitocris. He was the last king of ancient Babylon and he reigned a short time during the life of Daniel. Some commentators date this chapter as more than twenty years after the end of Daniel 4. There was certainly a time cap because Belshazzar does not know Daniel personally. Belshazzar was a very evil king and Dan. 5:1 says, "King Belshazzar gave a great banquet for a thousand of his nobles and drank wine with them." Life is fragile and the pagan mindset says, "Let us eat, drink, and be merry for tomorrow we will die" (Luke 22:19). For Belshazzar, it would not be tomorrow, it will be today.

Daniel 5 is like seeing a catastrophic tsunami coming and not being able to do anything about it. Sin is deceptive and it will cost Belshazzar his life and his kingdom. While Belshazzar was drinking his wine, he gave orders to bring in the gold and silver vessels that had been taken by Nebuchadnezzar from the temple in Jerusalem (vs. 2). These were holy vessels and were brought in "that the king and his lords, his wives, and his concubines might drink from them" (vs. 2). The true God was being mocked and rejected. Vs. 5 says, "As they drank the wine, they praised the gods of gold and silver, bronze and iron, wood and stone." When wine controls us, we always act the part of the fool. Is. 5:11 says, "Woe to those who rise early in the morning that they may pursue strong drink, who stay up late in the evening that wine may inflame them."

Belshazzar's goal was to demonstrate the superiority of the Babylonian gods over the God of the Hebrews. This foolish attempt to mock God will be a costly mistake. Gal. 6:7 says, "Do not be deceived, God is not mocked." The Greek word "mukterizo" literally means 'to turn up one's nose' and pictures the idea of scorn. The Message Bible says, "Don't be misled: No one makes a fool of God." Vs. 8 then says, "For the one who sows to his own flesh shall from the flesh reap corruption." The word "corruption" means "decay." This is not a sudden destruction brought about by external violence but an ending brought about by internal decay. Belshazzar and his guests were boldly practicing without shame idolatry. This, in turn, is almost always associated with immorality and other gross sins.

When you have a god of your own making, you have no accountability and easily give yourself over to the immoral passing pleasures of the world. This feast of wickedness and blasphemy where they praised the gods of their own making shows the serious moral decline of the great Babylonian empire. Not only did they show contempt of God by drinking from His holy vessels, they mock God by using them in the worship of idols. This is a praise service that will have a bad ending. Phil. 3:19 (NLT) says, "They are headed for destruction. Their god is their appetite, they brag about shameful things, and they think only about this life here on the earth." TPT, "Doom awaits them. Their god has possessed them and made them mute. Their boast is in their shameful lifestyles and their minds are in the dirt."

Belshazzar is about to have the surprise of his life. Yes, God is a patient God but He has His limits. As James 5:9 says, "The Judge is standing at the door." Eccl. 8:11 says, "Because the sentence against an evil deed is not executed quickly, therefore the hearts of the sons of men among them are given fully to do evil." In His mercy God may allow men to continue in their sin for a time but eventually there is a time for judgment. Num. 32:23, "Be sure your sin will find you out." 1 Thess. 5:3 says, "While they are saying, 'Peace and safety!' their destruction will come upon them suddenly like labor pains upon a woman with child, and they will not escape." With this sin of blasphemy against God, Belshazzar had crossed the line much like Ananias and Sapphira did when they lied to the Holy Spirit (Acts 5:3).

They both died immediately when their sin was found out. God is a holy God and He detests and has a feeling of repulsion over bold, flagrant sin. Their level of deceit was to deceive the Holy Spirit in front of the church and to make themselves look more spiritual than they actually were. Clearly their hearts were not right. They not only lied to the people but also to God who judged them with the strictest judgment. He struck them dead one at a time. Acts 5:11, "Great fear seized the whole church." This couple were judged quickly and harshly because

God wanted to make sure the church moved forward in the fear of the Lord. Just because we are living under the mercy seat of Christ doesn't mean we should no longer fear God. For sure, God is not a force to be reckoned with.

Dan. 5:5 says, "Suddenly the fingers of a man's hand appeared and wrote on the plaster of the wall, near the lampstand in the royal palace." God can and sometimes does communicate with people in unexpected and even shocking ways. Here, a hand mysteriously appeared and wrote on a wall. "Then the king's countenance changed, and his thoughts troubled him, so that the joints of his hips were loosened and his knees knocked against each other" (vs. 6). The ESV says "his color changed" and the NLT says "his face turned pale with fright." How quickly the swagger and boastfulness of sinners wilt in the presence of God. Matthew Henry said, "God's written word is enough to put the proudest, boldest sinner in fright. In a moment God can make the heart of the stoutest sinner to tremble."

This feast of blasphemy and immoral self-indulgence where the king had the audacity to mock God suddenly became a feast of gloom and fearful panic. Belshazzar was frightened out of his mind and he called all his astrologers and soothsayers to read the writing on the wall and give him its interpretation. They could not read or interpret the writing and vs. 9 says, "Then King Belshazzar was greatly troubled, his face grew more pale, and his nobles were astonished." Due to the noise caused by the king and his lords the queen came to the banquet hall and said, "O king, live forever! Do not let your thoughts trouble you." In essence she was saying, "Pull yourself together!" It is a bit of divine irony that she would tell him to live forever for he would not even live through that very night.

| 14 |

"VESSEL OF HONOR"

King Belshazzar was greatly troubled because he saw the hand of God mysteriously appear and write something on the wall that was not in his native language. He promised a great reward and promotion to anyone who could read and interpret this writing but none of his astrologers and soothsayers could do it. There will be moments in time when the world does not have the answers for what they're facing and they'll look for men of excellence to come and make sense of it all. People get desperate when they're in a desperate situation. This is when they look for the men of God to help them out. Stay full of the spirit of excellence and God will use you. As the king was shaking in his boots, the queen remembered what Daniel had done in the past and said, "There is a man in your kingdom in whom is the Spirit of the Holy God" (Dan. 4:11).

It is a testimony to Daniel's excellent spirit that the queen knew there was something different about him, something divine that no other person in the kingdom had. "And in the days of your father, light and understanding and wisdom, like the wisdom of the gods, were found in him" (vs. 11). Even unbelievers can recognize superior wisdom. All men need to be beacons of light in their Christian witness so that those lost in moral corruption and spiritual darkness will know a man of excellence is in their midst. God once encouraged the prophet Ezekiel, saying, "I am sending you to them who are impudent and stubborn children, and you shall say to them, 'Thus says the Lord God.' As for them, whether they listen or not - for they are a rebellious house - they will know that a prophet has been among them" (Ezek. 2:4,5).

It is a morally dark night in Babylon. The king has willfully and openly mocked and blasphemed God by drinking wine from the sacred vessels taken from the temple in Jerusalem. Yet in the midst of this gross darkness was the light of a man of excellence, a man who feared Belshazzar so little because he feared God so much. The queen continued, "This was because an excellent spirit, knowledge and insight, interpretation of dreams, solving riddles and explaining enigmas were found in this Daniel" (vs. 12). Notice that the queen referred to Daniel by his Jewish name, thus showing respect for his faith and heritage. There is no doubt his reputation was great among the pagans. 1 Peter 2:12 says, "Keep your behavior excellent among the Gentiles." The TPT says, "Live honorable lives as you mix with unbelievers, even though they accuse you of being evildoers."

Knowing what Daniel had done in the past by interpreting the dream of Nebuchadnezzar, the queen said, "Now let Daniel be called, and he will give the interpretation" (vs. 13). The soul of

Belshazzar plummeted into a hopeless sense of bewilderment. He was greatly afraid and very desperate and calling on Daniel was the last resort. His advisers were unable to help him so he was now ready to listen to anybody who could help him, even a Jewish man from the far away city of Jerusalem. What a tragedy that the ruler of the mighty city of Babylon should ignore one of the greatest men in history and turn to him only in the last hours of his life when it was too late. Daniel was brought before the king who asked him, "Are you that Daniel who is one of the exiles from Judah, whom my father the king brought from Judah?" (vs. 13).

The king continued, "I have heard of you, that the Spirit of God is in you, and that light, insight, understanding, and excellent wisdom are found in you" (vs. 14). Belshazzar knew about Daniel and the power he had to live an excellent life. To his shame he did not know Daniel personally nor did he know his God. For sure, Daniel was "a vessel of honor, sanctified, useful to the Master, prepared for every good work" (2 Tim. 2:21). God always has His people at the right place and the right time. Ray Pritchard said, "We never know our influence until a crisis comes. Soon enough life will come tumbling down and the people who have no time for you will turn to you for answers. You may not be invited to every party, but you will get the call when trouble comes. Never underestimate the power of a godly life."

When called upon, men of excellence must come forth fearlessly, asking only to be a vessel through which divine wisdom can be shared with a hurting and troubled world. Belshazzar explains the problem to Daniel and the failure of his wise men. They could not explain the writing because it was a supernatural message and they were natural men (vs. 15). God's supernatural revelation cannot be understood with natural intellect. 1 Cor. 2:14, "But a natural man does not accept the things of the Spirit of God, for they are foolishness to him." The king said if Daniel could make the interpretation known to him, he would be "clothed in purple and wear a necklace of gold around his neck and shall be the third ruler in the kingdom" (vs. 16). Daniel answered the king, "Keep your gifts for yourself or give your rewards to another; yet I will read the writing to the king, and make known the interpretation known to him" (vs. 17).

One thing about Daniel's excellence of spirit is that even when he's dealing with the miraculous and the prophetic there is within him a quiet, assured way of doing things. He is completely free of pride and arrogance for in him is a humble, devout, gracious, and heavenly spirit, a spirit of zeal for the glory of God and the good of all men. If we are going to minister in the things of God, particularly in challenging circumstances like this one, we need to have a simplicity of spirit. Daniel was straight forward when he talked to the king and he quickly cleared away the clutter in the king's thinking that caused him to be troubled. 1 Cor. 14:33 says, "For God is not a God of confusion but of peace." Simplicity is worth pursuing because it unlocks clarity and minimizes the distractions of life.

Simplicity is both discipline and a grace. Russian writer Leo Tolstoy once said, "There is no greatness where there is no simplicity, goodness, and truth." Dietrich Bonhoeffer said, "To be simple is to fix one's eye solely on the simple truth of God at a time when all concepts are being turned upside down." In 2 Cor. 11:3 Paul said he was concerned that anyone might beguile us so that our "minds may be corrupted from the simplicity that is in Christ." Here is Daniel tapping into that simplicity of spirit, that calm, quiet way of doing things. He had wisdom from above that is pure, peaceable, and gentle (James 3:17). He knows that anybody who puts selfish ambition on the throne of their life will have wisdom not from God but wisdom that is "earthly, sensual, and demonic" (James 3:15).

Daniel refused the king's reward for interpreting the writing on the wall because he didn't want to get caught up in the sin of selfish ambition. Having this same mentality will set us free so that we can tap into the wisdom of God and bring right words into the situation facing us. He was saying, "Let's get one thing settled before I speak. I am not here for the purple robe or the chain of gold around my neck or to be third ruler in the kingdom." He knew if these rewards was what he was after he wouldn't be able to tap into the wisdom of God and the interpretation would be of his own making and not from God. If you want to release the revelation of God in any given situation, you must clear away the clutter of selfish ambition and go about doing what God wants you to do.

Along with selfish ambition is the desire to make yourself look good. That's the root of pride and arrogance which will surely lead to your downfall. Phil. 2:5,7 says, "Let this mind be in you which was also in Christ Jesus who made Himself of no reputation, taking the form of a servant and coming in the likeness of men." We need to tap into the spirit of excellence which was in Christ. He left more in heaven than what He was ever offered on earth and He did everything with a spirit of humility. He went so far to say in Matt. 20:28, "For even the Son of Man did not come to be served, but to serve, and to give His life as a ransom for many." When you walk in simplicity and clear away the clutter of selfish ambition, you'll have a heart to serve the Lord and He will indeed use you in a mighty way.

Daniel is not interested in the temporal reward from a pagan king who that very night mocked and insulted the God of heaven in the most daring manner. One is reminded of Abram's refusal to accept gifts from the king of Sodom (Gen. 14:21-24) and Elisha's refusal of the offer of gifts by the Syrian Namaan (2 Kings 5:15,16). God's men cannot be bought off by offering them the passing pleasures of this present evil age. Daniel would not be deterred from speaking the absolute divine truth. A lesser man might have been induced and prevailed upon by the huge reward or intimidated by the threat of the king's vengeance. But not Daniel for in him was a spirit of excellence. With Belshazzar and a thousand drunken dignitaries as his audience, Daniel knew he wasn't just standing before the king of Babylon, he was standing before the King of kings.

With God as our audience and Christ as our companion, we have no reason to fear. Ps. 119:46 says, "I will also speak of Your testimonies before kings and shall not be ashamed." Daniel proceeds to give Belshazzar a short history lesson followed by a prophetic warning. His message was short but not sweet. It was forceful and very penetrating. Before giving the interpretation, Daniel first reminded the king how Nebuchadnezzar before him was given by the Most High God a kingdom and majesty, glory, and honor. "But when his heart was lifted up and his spirit became so proud that he behaved arrogantly, he was deposed from his royal throne and his glory was taken away from him" (vs. 20). Daniel reminds them that because of pride Nebuchadnezzar went insane for seven years and ate grass like oxen and his body became wet with the dew of heaven.

There is a saying that those who forget history are doomed to repeat it. Daniel is telling Belshazzar that he is doing the same thing Nebuchadnezzar did. He said, "But you, his son, Belshazzar, have not humbled your heart even though you knew all this. And you have lifted yourself up against the Lord of heaven" (vs. 22.23). Belshazzar knew what happened to Nebuchadnezzar and he should have known better. All people are responsible to honor God according to what revelation they have of Him. Rom. 2:5 says, "But because of your stubbornness and unrepentant heart you are storing up wrath for yourself in the day of wrath and revelation of the righteous judgment of God." Belshazzar knew what happened to his grandfather but did not heed the warning. He did not learn from history and blatantly refused to humble himself before God.

God expects men to respond to the light He gives them. When they do not, judgment is the only alternative. Belshazzar knew about God but in his pride defiantly rejected Him. Jesus said in

Luke 12:47, "And that slave who knew his master's will and did not get ready or act in accord with his will, will receive many lashes." Belshazzar had been exposed to the light of Nebuchadnezzar's humbling and exaltation of God. Greater light when ignored always brings a greater degree of judgment. Daniel charged Belshazzar with exalting himself above the Lord of heaven. He did not humble himself, he drank wine from holy vessels, and he worshiped idols. The final charge against Belshazzar was the most severe of all, "And the God who holds your breath in His hand and owns all your ways, you have not glorified" (vs. 23).

"Then the fingers of the hand were sent from Him, and this writing was written. And this is the inscription that was written: MENE, MENE, TEKEL, UPHARSIN. This is the interpretation of each word. MENE: God has numbered the days of your reign and brought it to an end" (vs. 24-26). God is saying, "I've got your number!" Charles Spurgeon said, "No man is out of the reach of the arrows of God." The word "MENE" appears twice for emphasis much like the doubling of Pharaoh's dream in Gen. 41:32. Belshazzar had crossed the line and there is no longer time for repentance. He was truly an irresponsible and reckless monarch. He had hardened his heart with pride. "TEKEL: You have been weighed on the scales and found wanting." God had weighed Belshazzar's life on the scales of justice and found that he came up short.

Hannah prayed in 1 Sam. 2:3, "Boast no more so very proudly. Do not let arrogance come out of your mouth, for the Lord is a God of knowledge, and with Him actions are weighed." Job knew that God would one day weigh our every thought, word, and action. He said in Job 31:6, "Let Him weigh me with accurate scales, and let God know my integrity." Belshazzar was "found wanting" because he had not fulfilled what God expected of him as an earthly ruler. He abused his position and failed to acknowledge and glorify God. "PERES: Your kingdom has been divided and given to the Medes and Persians." Notice Daniel did not say this division would one day happen. No, he speaks as if it already has happened. So certain is the judgment of God it may have been happening as they were speaking.

Sad to say, Belshazzar did not repent which would have honored God. Instead, he honored Daniel by giving him the rewards he originally offered to whoever gave the interpretation. He ordered Daniel to be clothed with a purple robe and to have a gold necklace put around his neck. He also gave him authority as third ruler in the kingdom (vs. 29). Most people would revere the thought of being promoted to a high position of authority but there are some promotions we do best to ignore and this is a prime example. Besides, Daniel held this position for only a few hours for the Babylonian empire came to an end that very night. This shows how temporary the awards and accolades of this world are. "That very night Belshazzar, king of the Chaldeans, was slain. And Darius the Mede received the kingdom, being about sixty-two years old" (vs. 30,31).

God's justice and judgment was swift and sure. Sinners like to believe that God will never punish them or, if He does, it will be far off in the distant future. They wrongly believe they'll have plenty of time to repent and get ready to meet the Lord. They don't realize there may come a time when God says, "You've crossed the line." The truth is that God is not obligated to continually send His Spirit to convict people of their sin. The time may come when the Holy Spirit no longer works in a person's heart. Heb. 10:26 (TPT) says, "For if we continue to persist in deliberate sin after we have known and received the truth, there is not another sacrifice to be made for us." It is foolish to presume the grace of God will always be there for us. It won't be. May we all learn that "it is a terrible thing to fall into the hands of the living God" (Heb. 10:31).

| 15 |

"TRUE GREATNESS"

Daniel 5 is in the Bible so we will know that what happened to Babylon can also happen to us. After all, our days on this planet are also numbered. Heb. 9:27 says, "And as it is appointed for men to die once, but after this the judgment." There are a predetermined number of days that you will live on the earth. This is not a discouraging thing if you're ready for what's on the other side. Men of excellence know that "to live is Christ and to die is gain" (Phil. 1:21). Actually, all people live forever. It's just that their time on earth is like "a vapor that appears for a little time and then vanishes away" (James 4:14). It's important to know your days are numbered because anything you think you have a lot of you tend to squander but anything you think you have a limited amount of you tend to use wisely.

Like Belshazzar your life will also be weighed on the scales of justice. This is why you can't live a carefree life thinking what you do doesn't matter. Whether you like it or not, one day you're going to stand before God and be judged. He'll look at you and say, "What did you do with the one life I gave you?" Are you like Belshazzar who squandered his life away or like Daniel who lived for the glory of God? Either way it will be revealed on your day of reckoning before God. Don't allow your life to get out of balance. Don't get out of bed saying, "Let the good times roll." Instead, seek to fulfill the will of God for your life each and every day. Turn off the television, put down your smart phone, put away your golf clubs. If you're burning the candle at both ends, you're not as bright as you think you are.

If you're too busy for God, you're too busy. Slow down and re-arrange your priorities. Eccl. 4:6 says, "It is better to have only a little with peace of mind than be busy all the time." Belshaz-zar's kingdom was divided and given to another. Likewise, if your life is not balanced, the devil will come in and bring divi-sion to your family, your health, and your peace. Don't ignore the warning signs. If you don't realize your days are numbered and if you don't get your life in order, everything that per-tains to your life will be divided. If you don't heed the warning signs, the risk of sinful choices increase. In other words, you'll be tempted to sin more often than you normally are. Jesus said in Matt. 10:28, "Don't fear those who can kill the body but are not able to kill the soul; rather fear Him who is able to destroy both soul and body in hell."

You can't have an excellent spirit with an earthly perspective. You've got to have a heavenly perspective. Jesus said we "are not of this world, even as I am not of it" (John 17:16). You'll be able to successfully navigate the shifting culture of today's society if you're not of this world. Get on God's side and you won't go down with the sinking ship. Paul said, "Many live as enemies of the cross of Christ. Their destiny is destruction, their god is their stomach, and their glory is their shame. Their mind is set on earthly things" (Phil. 3:18,19). Paul is saying people follow their feelings. Whatever their body tells them to do, they do it. Their feelings and sensual appetites have become a god to them. Notice what Paul says next, "But our citizenship is in heaven. And we eagerly await a Savior from there, the Lord Jesus Christ" (vs. 20). This world is not our home. We're just passing through.

The disciples once went to Jesus and they were greatly discouraged. Jesus said to them, "Let not your heart be troubled. In My Father's house are many mansions" (John 14:1,2). His solution to their earthly problems is to have a heavenly perspective. This is why Paul said, "Set your mind on things above, not on things on the earth" (Col. 3:2). TPT, "Yes, feast on all the treasures of the heavenly realm and fill your thoughts with heavenly realities and not with the distractions of the natural realm." This is how Daniel lived his life. If you'll live the same way, you'll step into today's culture change filled with courage. How do you stay steady when everything is falling apart? Danish theologian Soren Kiesegaard said in the 19th century, "By means of the eternal one can conquer the future, because the eternal is the foundation of the future."

Go through life looking up where God is and not around you where the devil is. Always focus on the eternal and not on the ever-changing temporal things of life. Jesus said in Luke 21:28,

"When these things begin to take place, stand up and lift up your heads, because your redemption is drawing near." To survive hard times and the changing conditions and the waves of life, the Message Bible says, "Stand tall with your head help high. Help is on the way!" Focus your life on the unseen things of God and not on the seen things of this world (2 Cor. 4:18). Rise up and do something eternal with your life, laying up for yourself treasures in heaven (Matt. 6:20). Don't focus on things that will eventually pass away, focus on the eternal things of God. Men and women of excellence are not intimidated by earthly treasures because their heart is in the hope of heaven.

Belshazzar is now dead and the mighty Babylonian empire has come to an end being divided between the Medes and Persians just like Nebuchadnezzar's dream predicted. Darius the Mede is now in charge and Dan. 6:1 says, "It pleased Darius to set over the kingdom one hundred and twenty satraps to be over the whole kingdom." The word "satrap" is a Persian word meaning 'protector of the realm.' They were chief representatives of the king and could also be called overseers and administrators. They were considered the eyes and ears of the king and had their own court and absolute civil authority over the province they were in charge of. Dan. 6:2 says Darius placed over these satraps "three governors of whom Daniel was one, that the satraps might give account to them, so that the king might suffer no loss."

Daniel is now about 80 years old and he worked for the government for many years. He was a man of character, a man of consistency, a man of conviction, and a man of courage. "Then this Daniel distinguished himself above the governors and satraps because an excellent spirit was in him, and the king planned to set him over the whole kingdom" (vs. 3). The word "distinguished" means 'successful, authoritative, and commanding great respect, showing dignity in one's appearance and manner.' If you want to have influence in a culture that is not your own, you can't reflect the culture, you've got to distinguish yourself and set a new culture for others to follow. You have to be different from everybody else. Why? Because you can't make a difference unless you are different. You can't change anything if you're like everyone else.

The Hebrew word for "distinguish" is "nesah" and one of the meanings of this word is 'brightness' or 'brilliance.' For sure, Daniel's spirit shone brightly in the darkness. Webster's 1828 dictionary says "distinguish" means 'to ascertain and indicate difference by some external mark, to separate one thing from another by some mark or quality.' What separated Daniel from the other governors was his excellent, outstanding, and superior spirit. Whatever he did exceeded the expectations of those around him. Darius recognized that Daniel was a rare jewel, a man of integrity, a blameless man who shined brightly in the midst of a crooked and perverse generation (Phil. 2:15). An ancient proverb says "integrity is the first step toward true greatness." Daniel was different and distinct. He had a good attitude and shined above the other two governors.

Your reputation is what people think you are while your character is what God knows you are. Daniel had both. He knew that what a man is in the sight of God is what he truly is. Integrity can be defined as the condition or quality of being un-divided. It describes those who adhere to their ethical or moral standards without hypocrisy or deceitfulness. Integrity means soundness, completeness, and honesty. Your integrity may be God's means of saving those around you. They'll be drawn to God as they observe your uprightness. Integrity shines bright-est against the backdrop of adversity. People may doubt what you say but they will always believe what you do. Spiritual in-tegrity calls for the highest possible standard of behavior. A person of integrity stands by their godly principles no matter the consequences.

Daniel had such exceptional qualities that the king planned to set him over the entire kingdom much like Pharaoh did with Joseph back in Egypt. In God's kingdom, it is only those with a spirit of excellence, those who distinguish themselves with ex-ceptional qualities, who are able to do great things for God. It is a certainty that if you don't have a God-like character and integrity, you won't be put in charge of anything. Like Daniel, live your life in such a way that gets people's attention. All the governors and satraps were jealous of the favor bestowed on Daniel so they "sought to find some charge against Daniel in his conduct of government affairs" (vs. 4). The twin sins of envy and jealousy, stirred by the devil, aroused these men to plot against Daniel. In this world, the man of integrity can be-come a target for those who lack integrity.

Let's not forget what the Bible says about jealousy. Song of Solomon 8:6 says jealousy is "as cruel as the grave; It's flames are flames of fire, a most vehement flame." As expected, their search to find something wrong with Daniel was in vain. "They could find no corruption in him, because he was faithful, nor was there any error or fault found in him" (vs. 4). Daniel's integrity was beyond question because he was faithful and trustworthy. No dark spots were found in his life because of his extraordinary spirit and his exceptional excellence. Daniel's life was blameless and without reproach, so much so that his accusers could find nothing wrong with him. He was loyal in his government duties all the while giving God first place. We learn from Daniel that if we call ourselves a person of excellence, we are bound to live in such a way that the world will have no doubt of the depth of our fellowship with the Lord above.

It is God's plan that all men and women rise up and make a positive difference in the world we live in. This will happen when we become like mirrors who brightly reflect the glory of God. 2 Cor. 3:18 says, "All of us reflect the Lord's glory with faces that are not covered with veils and are being changed into His image with ever-increasing glory." Having unveiled faces means we have direct access to God. We then enter into a process where we get transformed into His image as we move from one brighter image of glory to another. In other words, men and women of excellence are to be "glow in the dark" believers, the type of person who makes it easier for those who walk in darkness to believe in God also. Consider Ps. 34:5 that says, "They looked to Him and were radiant and their faces will never be ashamed." TPT, "Gaze upon Him, join your life with His. Your face will glisten with glory."

The more we look like Christ, the more the world will want what we have. The clearest picture of the image and glory of God that we are to reflect is found in heaven before the throne of God. John had a vision of the throne of God and said, "In the center, around the throne, were four living creatures, and they were covered with eyes, in front and in back. The first living creature was like a lion, the second was like an ox, the third had a face like a man, the fourth was like a flying eagle" (vs. 6,7). The prophet Ezekiel saw these same creatures in Ezek. 1:10 but he goes on to say in vs. 28, "This was the appearance of the likeness of the glory of the Lord." Most Bible scholars believe this is an actual representation of what God looks like. Therefore, if God looks like these four faces, then you are to look like them also.

What does God look like? What are you to look like? The face of an ox represents the face of a servant. The ox served the farmer as it helped plow his fields and pull heavy loads. Jesus came to the earth and "made Himself of no reputation and took upon Him the form of a servant" (Phil. 2:7). Daniel also was a servant making sure the king suffered no loss (Dan. 6:2). The way to people's hearts is not to judge them but to serve them. It's when you deny and set aside all your rights in order to serve other people and put them first. All men and women of excellence must have the face of a servant. 1 Cor. 9:19 says, "Though I am free and belong to no man, I make myself a servant to all, that I might win the more." This is how you change the world. This is how you lead many to the Lord. Martin Luther once said, "A Christian man is a ministering servant in all things, subject to everybody."

Next, the face of a man is the face of love. People of the world don't want a doctrinal debate with you. No, they want to know God loves them and they find that out by you loving them. People don't care how much of the Bible you know, they want to know that you care about them with a sincere heart of love, a never-ending love that always seek their well-being. Jesus said, "A new command I give you: Love one another. As I have loved you, so you must love one another. By this all men will know you are My disciples, if you love one another" (John 13:34,35). Before you give advice to people on how to solve their problems, show them first that you love them, that you really, truly do care about them and what they're going through. We walk in love by imitating God the Father just like Jesus did. Eph. 5:1,2 says, "Be imitators of God, as beloved children. And walk in love, as Christ loved us and gave Himself up for us."

Third, the face of an eagle is the face of respect, the face of dignity and honor. A bald eagle is majestic and commands the respect of everyone who gazes upon it. God wants you to live your life in such a way that people will look at you and say, "Wow! That's impressive! I have never seen a person do things like you do them." About Jesus Mark 7:37 says, "And they were overwhelmed with amazement, saying, 'He has done all things well.'" They were astonished beyond measure and all of them said, "Wow!" They said this about Jesus and God wants them to say the same thing about you. Matt. 5:13 says, "You are the salt of the earth." Every place you go you are to make life taste better. Trust God and He will use you to make people excited and get them interested in the things of God. When you love and serve people, your life will continually be full of "wow" moments.

Finally, the face of a lion is the face of boldness. The world will tell you to be quiet in what you believe in but men and women of excellence are relentless in proclaiming the goodness of God. They stand firm in the faith while others of lesser or no faith flee. Prov. 28:1 says, "The wicked flee when no one pursues, but the righteous are bold as a lion." Don't be rude but be bold and speak the truth in love (Eph. 4:15). Boldness is the courage to act or speak fearlessly. When a person acts boldly, they take action regardless of risk. Boldness will empower you to do or speak what is necessary. The disciples prayed in Acts 4:29, "Lord, grant to Your servants that with all boldness they may speak Your word." God gives us boldness when our objective is to obey and glorify Him with it. This is why Jesus was so bold and Daniel also. May this same boldness be in you as well.

| 16 |

"WORTH DYING FOR"

D aniel was a man with an excellent spirit and he distinguished himself above the other government officials chosen by King Darius to rule in his kingdom. He was highly favored and this sparked the fire of jealousy in the hearts of the other administrators, so much so that they sought means to destroy this man of integrity. What put Daniel in the crosshairs of his enemies is his faith. All his life he kept himself unstained by the pagan, idolatrous, and immoral culture in which he lived. There were no skeletons in Daniel's closet and, as hard as they tried, these officials could find nothing wrong to charge him with. The only alternative was to make something up. Then these men said, "We shall not find any charge against this Daniel unless it has something to do with the law of his God" (Dan. 6:5).

They knew Daniel well for his profession of faith was well known. They knew he could not be trapped into doing evil and would be faithful to his God in all circumstances. Daniel was truly an exceptional man and did not hide his faith in the one true God. No wonder Ezekiel ranked him with Noah and Job as the most godly of men (Ezek. 14:14). The only way to harm Daniel and get him out of the way would be to devise a plot wherein he was forced to choose between obedience to God and obedience to Mede-Persian law. Daniel was a righteous man and was not ashamed to be seen praying to his God. This, then, became the means by which they would take him down. Or so they thought. These officials knew Daniel but they also knew King Darius. They knew they could appeal to his pride and arrogance so as a group they went to him and said, "King Darius, live forever!" (vs. 6).

Over one hundred and twenty of these officials now have the king's attention and they will use manipulation, flattery, and deceit in their effort to take down the man of God. Ps. 2:1,2 asks the question, "Why do the nations rage, and the people plot a vain thing? The kings of the earth and the rulers take counsel together against the Lord and against His anointed." An unholy conspiracy is about to take place as they tell the king they have all consulted together and are in agreement with what they're about to ask him to do. This is an outright lie because Daniel was a governor and he had not been consulted. It is also interesting to note that Darius did not notice that Daniel was not among those standing before him. These evil men set out to flatter the ambition of the king as they suggested he pass a 30-day law forbidding any person from praying to anyone except to Darius himself.

They flattered Darius with the idea that he could be a god for a month. Flattery is the art of telling a person exactly what he thinks of himself which explains why it is so effective. John MacArthur said, "Ancient kings were frequently worshiped as gods. Pagans had such inferior views of their gods that such homage was no problem." They knew Daniel would never agree to this law so they said, "Whoever petitions any god or man for thirty days, except you, O king, shall be cast into the den of lions. Now, O king, establish the decree and sign the writing, so that it cannot be changed, according to the law of the Medes and Persians, which may not be revoked" (vs. 7,8). "Therefore King Darius signed the written decree" (vs. 9). It has well been said that flattery is manipulation, not communication. In his pride, Darius succumbed to the flattery of evil men.

Dan. 6:10 says, "Now when Daniel knew that the writing was signed, he went home." He did not deliberate a single minute but did as was his custom since the early days. "And in his upper room, with his windows open toward Jerusalem, he knelt down on his knees three times that day and prayed and gave thanks before his God" (vs. 10). Charles Spurgeon said, "Not one jot of anxiety did he betray. His faith was steadfast, his composure unruffled, his conduct simple and artless." It is the sworn duty of every man of God to disregard every law on earth which is contrary to the law of heaven. Peter said, "We ought to obey God rather than man" (Acts 5:29). Daniel served loyally before King Darius, yet he knew the King of kings deserved a higher loyalty. He refused to give Darius the measure of obedience that belonged to God alone.

Some would say Daniel put his life on the line by disobeying the written decree, but he knew the safest thing he could do was radically obey God. Dr. Martin Luther King Jr. once said, "If a man hasn't discovered something that he will die for, he isn't fit to live." Indeed, Daniel discovered something worth dying for. This is why without hesitation he knelt down on his knees, praying like Jesus did (Luke 22:41), like Stephen (Acts 7:60), like Peter (Acts 9:40), and like Paul (Acts 20:36). He prayed three times that day and gave thanks because great prayer is filled with thanksgiving. He gave thanks all the while knowing his next appointment will be the den of lions. This beloved prophet is kneeling in sweet communion with his Lord. When one knows how to kneel in prayer, he has no problem standing firm against opposition when it comes.

As planned, these officials who plotted against Daniel found him praying and making supplication before his God (vs. 11). In other words, they found him breaking the law of the land. They then went and informed King Darius what they had found, telling him that "Daniel, who is one of the captives from Judah, does not show due regard for you" (vs. 13). This was not true. Daniel intended no disrespect for the king, only a higher respect for God. When Darius heard these words he "was greatly distressed with himself" (vs. 14). Darius liked Daniel and he now recognized that he had been deceived by the lies of these jealous officials. But instead of blaming others, he knew he was at fault. His foolish decree haunted him and he "set his heart on Daniel to deliver him; and he labored till the going down of the sun to deliver him" (vs. 14).

The officials would not allow this to happen and reminded the king "that no decree or statute which the king establishes may be changed" (vs. 15). Then the king gave orders, and Daniel was brought in and cast into the den of lions. The king spoke and said to Daniel, "Your God, whom you serve continually, He will deliver you" (vs. 16). Darius had faith that was born out of Daniel's trust in the Lord. He was saying, "I tried my best to save you Daniel, but I failed. Now it is up to your God." A stone was brought and laid over the mouth of the den and the king sealed it with his own signet ring so that nothing would be changed in regard to Daniel (vs. 17). The heart of Darius was greatly burdened and he "went off to the palace and spent the night fasting and his sleep fled from him" (vs. 18). He could not sleep while Daniel slept like a baby.

Morning couldn't get here fast enough for King Darius. When it did arrive "the king arose very early in the morning and went in haste to the den of lions" (vs. 19). With a grieving, troubled voice he called out, "Daniel, servant of the living God, has your God, whom you serve continually, been able to deliver you from the lions?" (vs. 20). Daniel's life of excellence was a shining light in a dark world and Darius recognized this. 2 Cor. 2:14 says God "manifests through us the sweet aroma of the knowledge of Him in every place." Daniel replied, "O king, live forever! My God sent His angel and shut the lions' mouths, so that they have not hurt me, because I was found innocent before Him" (vs. 21,22). These words made the king exceedingly glad and he gave orders for Daniel to be taken up out of the den. "No injury whatever was found on him because he believed in his God" (vs. 23).

"The king then gave orders, and they brought those men who had maliciously accused Daniel, and they cast them, their children and their wives into the lions' den" (vs. 24). This is the law of sowing and reaping in action. Ps. 7:15,16 says about the wicked, "He made a pit and has fallen into the ditch he made. His trouble shall return upon his own head." The guilty are now punished in place of the innocent. "And the lions overpowered them, and broke all their bones into pieces before they ever came to the bottom of the den" (vs.24). When all was said and done, King Darius made a decree that in all the dominion of his kingdom men are to fear and tremble before the God of Daniel. The last thing the Bible says about Daniel is that he "prospered in the reign of Darius and in the reign of Cyrus the Persian" (vs. 28). Such is the life of a man of excellence.

In the story of Daniel, the one thing that always shines through is his inner peace. No matter what he went through, he always grabbed hold of the peace that comes from knowing God is on your side. Peace is a condition of freedom from disturbance whether outwardly or inwardly. God's peace is that tranquil state of a soul that is assured of its salvation through Christ. Phil. 4:6,7 (GWT) says, "Be anxious for nothing. Then God's peace, which goes beyond anything we can imagine, will guard your hearts and emotions through Christ Jesus." The peace of God replaces anxiety in the life of the prayerful believer. It is not the absence of problems but a reflection of divine sufficiency in the midst of adversity. Is. 26:3 says, "The steadfast of mind You will keep in perfect peace, because he trusts in You." In other words, "If God be for us, who can be against us?" (Rom. 8:31).

The peace of God is beyond our comprehension for we cannot fully understand it, yet it is not beyond our experience for we can walk in it every day of our lives. Pastor Dwight Edwards said, "If the peace of God is not ruling or standing sentry over our inner man, then an unwanted intruder has already entered in." Peace is a state of tranquility or quietness of spirit that rises above our circumstances. It is a gift from God and is in complete harmony with His character. Living in peace can be compared to the petals of a flower unfolding in the morning sunlight when we refuse to allow our circumstances to determine our level of contentment. The man who places his full confidence in a loving God and is thankful in every situation will possess a supernatural peace. For sure, an inner calm will dominate his heart.

When the storms of life are raging around them, when the wind blows and the waves roar, men and women of excellence have an obligation to let their hearts be guided by the peace of the Anointed One. Jesus gives His disciples peace based on the truth that He has overcome the world (John 16:33). When we allow the Spirit of God to rule in our lives, we will experience His peace. The peace of God is unconditional and can be experienced even in difficult times. It's a peace that surpasses all understanding and can guard your heart and your mind. From the beginning of time people have pursued happiness at all costs. Everyone wants to be happy but continue to struggle to find the secret to true happiness. They struggle because what they really want is peace and not happiness. Peace is eternal but happiness is always changing with situations in life and fickle emotions.

Peace makes us content and happy in all situations. It's a fruit of the Spirit and is not found in the material things of this world, things such as power, fame, and money. Those who achieve the best things this world has to offer still feel an emptiness down inside of them. Yes, they're happy for a while but the lack of peace leaves a void in their inner man. That feeling of emptiness is there because true peace and contentment is something only God can give. C. S. Lewis said, "God cannot give us a happiness and peace apart from Himself." There is no such thing as true peace without God. He is peace and in Him you find all the answers you're searching for. He is the fulfillment of everything you're looking for. Jesus said in John 14:27, "Peace I leave with you, My peace I give to you; not as the world gives do I give to you. Let not your heart be troubled, neither let it be afraid."

New life in God doesn't keep you from all the problems of this world. You will have trials and tribulations. The difference is you can now have peace in hard times. Jesus said, "These things I have spoken to you, that in Me you may have peace. In the world you will have tribulation but be of good cheer, I have overcome the world" (John 16:33). Paul said in 2 Thess. 3:16, "Now may the Lord of peace Himself give you peace always in every way. The Lord be with you all." The MSG says He is "the Master of Peace." If you are a person of excellence who walks in the Spirit, you will always experience peace even in difficult times. It's a fruit of the Spirit (Gal. 5:22) and is forever inside of you. To experience the divine peace of God you must let the Holy Spirit lead you and guide you. If you let Him guide your emotions, your intellect, and your will, you will always have peace.

This peace doesn't come from material things or from yourself, it comes only from God. Col. 3:15 (NLT) says, "And let the peace that comes from Christ rule in your hearts." Not only will this peace that comes from God help you to handle everything life throws at you, you'll also be a bright light to the world around you. May you always shine that light. Jesus said in Matt. 5:14,15, "You are the light of the world. A city that is set on a hill cannot be hidden nor do people light a lamp and put it under a basket." He then said in vs. 16, "Let your light shine before men, that they may see your good works and glorify your Father in heaven." People of excellence always shine bright. You need to understand that going through difficult times can be an opportunity where God wants to use you as His light to shine forth the truth of how good He is.

We can have peace because Rom. 8:28 promises us that God will let all things work together for our good. Men and women of excellence always see the bigger plan of God. Walk with God "and always be ready to make a defense to anyone who asks for a reason for the hope that is in you; and do it with gentleness and respect" (1 Peter 3:15). People need to see the light in you because they're living in darkness like you once lived in darkness. With peace you can endure hardships for the sake of Christ. Have peace knowing that your trials may be the stepping stone necessary to put you where God wants you to be. He wants you at a certain place at a certain time so He can use you. As you go through these hard times, remember Ps. 37:3,

"Trust in the Lord, and do good; Dwell in the land, and feed on His faithfulness." For sure, He will never let you down.

1 Cor. 10:13 says, "God is faithful and will not let you be tempted beyond your ability, but with the temptation He will also provide the way of escape, that you may be able to endure it." Trust God always knowing there is nothing beyond His control. It is a beautiful thing to trust God at all times. When you do that, He'll give you supernatural peace that passes all understanding. Perfect, absolute peace surrounds those whose imaginations are consumed with God. When you trust God, you will taste and see that He is good (Ps. 34:8). Peace comes when you know that your life, your circumstances, and your future are in the loving and capable and merciful hands of the Lord above. Since God has promised to stand by your side forevermore you can have the faith of Abraham to whom the Lord said, "Do not fear for I am a shield to you; Your reward shall be very great" (Gen. 15:1).

SUMMARY

As we close our journey through the first six chapters of Daniel, we are left with a portrait of a man whose life stood as a beacon of faithfulness in a faithless world. From his youth in Babylon to his years of high authority under foreign kings, Daniel's story reminds us that true greatness is not found in power, prestige, or position, but in steadfast devotion to God.

Daniel's unwavering resolve began in chapter one, where he purposed in his heart not to defile himself. That single decision set the tone for the rest of his life. It was a quiet act of obedience, yet it became the foundation for every victory that followed. The same God who honored Daniel's faith in the small things was the One who sustained him through trials of fire, fury, and fear.

In the fiery furnace, we witnessed the faith of his friends - Shadrach, Meshach, and Abednego - who refused to bow to idols, confident that even if deliverance did not come, they would still remain true to God. In the lion's den, we saw Daniel's unshakable trust and prayerful consistency, proving that no law of man can silence the voice of a heart devoted to the Lord. In every test, God's sovereignty was revealed, His faithfulness confirmed, and His glory magnified.

The book of Daniel is not merely a record of ancient miracles but a divine testimony to the enduring power of faith. It calls each believer to live with conviction in the midst of compromise, courage in the face of danger, and consistency when the world demands conformity. Daniel's life teaches us that when we stand firm for God, heaven stands with us.

As we step away from these pages, may we carry Daniel's example into our own generation. May we, too, purpose in our hearts to remain faithful no matter the cost, to pray even when it is unpopular, to trust when it seems impossible, and to shine when darkness surrounds us. The God who shut the lions' mouths still reigns today, and He is still looking for men and women like Daniel—those whose faith will not bow, whose hope will not waver, and whose lives will glorify His name in every season.

Let us, therefore, dare to live as Daniel lived - faithful, fearless, and full of God's favor - until the kingdoms of this world become the Kingdom of our Lord and of His Christ.

www.ingramcontent.com/pod-product-compliance
Lightning Source LLC
Chambersburg PA
CBHW070924130626
46555CB00001B/275